AT HOME

A Client's Appreciation
for Authentic Architecture

AT HOME

A Client's Appreciation
for Authentic Architecture

by DEBORAH LENCIONI LAPP

photos by   Scot Zimmerman

foreword by   Arthur Dyson, FAIA

ORGANIC ARCHITECTURE AND DESIGN ARCHIVES, INC.   OA+D ARCHIVES PRESS   ARIZONA   2023

Published in the United States by OA+D Archives Press, a division of Organic Architecture + Design Archives, Inc., Chandler, Arizona.

www.oadarchives.org

ISBN: 978-1-938938-71-9

LCCN: 2023942462

Book design by Eric O'Malley

Printed and bound in the United States of America

Previous Spread: *Lapp RiverHouse (designed by Arthur Dyson).*
Front Cover: *The Creek House (Arthur Dyson's Lencioni Residence).*
Back Cover: *Lapp RiverHouse (designed by Arthur Dyson).*
All photos by David Swann, post-production by Susan R. Thompson.

For my husbands, who spring my dreams to life:
Greg Alan Lapp
Dennis Lencioni (1954–2003)

Deb and Greg Lapp at the RiverHouse.
Photo by Amy Roberts.

Dennis Lencioni at the Creek House.
Photo courtesy of the author.

Rationalists, wearing square hats,

Think, in square rooms,

Looking at the floor.

Looking at the ceiling.

They confine themselves To right-angled triangles.

If they tried rhomboids,

Cones, waving lines. ellipses—

As, for examples, the ellipses of the half-moon—

Rationalists would wear sombreros.

—Wallace Stevens,
from *Six Significant Landscapes (no. VI)*

Above: *Lencioni Residence dining area.*
Photo courtesy of the author.

CONTENTS

FOREWORD

Arthur Dyson, FAIA

Above: *Audrey Dyson, Arthur Dyson, and Deborah Lencioni Lapp.*
Photo by David Swann.

F or an architect, one of the happiest signs of a well-served client is a return with another commission. In the case of Deborah Lapp and her family, I have had the pleasure and privilege of serving their architectural needs multiple times. Two of these projects produced houses that continue to support active and engaged lives. This accomplishment is due in substantial measure to thoughtful awareness and willing self-examination of an articulate client committed to exploring the potential of architecture to realize an adventuresome vision for personal and community life. In the present book, she shares the course of her decades-long experience of rendering intangible wishes, needs, and qualities into useful and efficient tangible forms. As an architect, I am deeply impressed with the depth of understanding she expresses about the process of architectural design.

As you read these pages, you will see the many considerations, explorations, aspirations, and experimental solutions that Deborah encountered throughout her journey of architectural realization. She recounts in a frank and intimate way both the joys and the frustrations of pursuing creative building design—and notes with conviction there is no going back once good results show the satisfactions that can be achieved. Her words come from the lived experience of dwelling consciously, negotiating and choosing carefully amid options and limitations, and deliberately making a creative pathway for herself, her family, and her community. Her book, like the houses she has chosen to build, is an offering of the heart to encourage others to take the road less traveled. In my good fortune of being her architect, I appreciate greatly the compliment Deborah pays to my services.

More importantly, however, I am very happy the journey continues to be shared. ▪

PREFACE:
WHY YOU'LL WANT
TO READ THIS BOOK

Above: *Awning over the Creek House deck.*
Photo courtesy of the author.

P otential clients of artist-architects: I've been where you are—three times, so I understand your reservations. Yet, if you value a stimulating environment as I do, I suggest it's worth the time and money, and (easily overlooked point) you can avoid spending as much money if you're willing to spend more time. Your home can precisely reflect your personality, your values, and your dreams and bring you closer to them. Yes, you can try this "at home"!

Students of architecture: It's only logical that you understand your clients' points of view since clients are the ones who will finance your art. You likely went into architecture in the first place because you dreamed of a soul-satisfying career. You chose architecture to create art, not human storage units. I urge you to pursue those dreams as you contribute to a society suffering from drab, soul-sapping efficiency.

Instructors of architecture: What do you teach about the client, the one who typically finances the project, but whose education in architecture and design is influenced by what he or she has seen in the media or by extant homes? Clients are easily influenced by arguments of "feasibility" and unaware of the consequences of compromise. Only through education by their architects will most understand the layers of benefit from authentically personalized design. Please guide your students in the skill of educating clients towards satisfying choices. This book could be a textbook.

Practicing architects: You know you have some stunningly creative work in your bottom drawer. You originally became an architect to create. I hope to embolden you and give you more of an idea of how clients might think and feel. Your clients don't have your knowledge or your ideas—that's why they come to you. Please teach them to care about artistic architecture. Please give them this book.

Builders and craftspeople: While it's comfortable and easier (and, okay, probably cheaper in many cases) to build the same design repeatedly, *it's to your benefit* to create inspiring and satisfying work. I'll argue that if you avoid cutting architectural corners, you'll attract better clients as a result. You'll be authentically proud of your legacy. You'll have a portfolio you're proud of. Look at what *you* built.

Artists of all stripes: It stands to reason that artists are inspired by this architecture. I have had the opportunity to know and to interview many artists who appreciate and are somehow involved in authentic architecture, especially Arthur Dyson. Dyson inspires people around him to drop everything and devote their lives to the pursuit of beauty. The stories here are both instructive and inspiring—and sometimes cautionary.

Enthusiasts of organic architecture and authentic design: While I struggle with what to call the architecture to which I refer, my examples are overwhelmingly organic and overwhelmingly the works of our architect Arthur Dyson. In his words: "It is this potential of improving the human condition that motivates me…it is the foundation built by my direct predecessors [his teachers] Frank Lloyd Wright, Bruce Goff, and William Gray Purcell, that has given me the platform to work for a more meaningful and humane architecture."

My dozen or so precious blog followers at *orgatecture.org*: I hope it was worth the wait. ▪

Above: *The author in front of Dyson's University High School.*
Photo by Greg Lapp.

INTRODUCTION:
WHY THE *CLIENT?*
MY ARCHITECTURAL HISTORY

Above: San Joaquin Valley in Fresno County, California.
Photo courtesy of the author.

"Our clients become true partners rather than masters or victims."

—Sim van der Ryn
in David Pearson's *New Organic Architecture*

am not an architect. Mine is a philosophy of architecture from a client's point of view. Having experienced joy, contentment, fulfillment, and trials over many projects and decades, I have found the difficulties involved are ultimately worth it. Because I am thrilled by artistic architecture, I'd like to see more of it in this world.

My experiences are limited to the San Joaquin Valley in Fresno County, where the summers are hot and dry, the winters cold and foggy, but rarely below freezing, but I have toured authentic, artistic, organic homes in wide-ranging regions.

Back in the mid-1980s, my late husband Dennis Lencioni and I were living in the downstairs apartment of a drafty duplex on the back side of a ranch with an absentee owner. We were in our twenties; he was a farrier, and I was in grad school. The brilliant aspect of our lodging was that it was rent-free in exchange for tending the cattle, which started us on a habit of radical saving and investment early on, which I have chosen to reinvest in architecture.

A long distance runner back then, I crested the hill one morning at Rio Vista, turned left onto Trimmer Springs Road, and spied my grandmother, Evelyn Ball, in her red sweatshirt with the hood up, looking for all the world like an elf, tying white bows around the oak trees.

As a wedding present, Gran, who lived on the ranch next door, gifted Dennis and me 7.6 acres of riverbottom land she told me she had wanted to build on in the 1960s, but was told it was unbuildable. My last semester, I spent more time drawing floor plans than studying or wedding planning. We would build.

Above: Morning jog: Dennis and Gran. Photo courtesy of the author.

Dennis was a pilot, so on weekends we circled around and around over the wooded wetland property looking for high ground.

He'd tip the plane sideways, and I'd take photos. We'd study how dark or light the foliage was—lighter, we deduced, meant drier. A tangle of blackberries and willows covered the creek and cloaked the forest as in a fairy tale, but it took more than love or magic to clear a path to the center where we correctly predicted we'd find high ground.

We started with machetes and a chainsaw, but quickly switched to a tractor with a pallet mower, backing in to devour the water willows and Himalayan blackberry. Scratched and sticky with plant sap and sweat, we'd proudly survey the few meager meters of progress we'd make in a day. Finally, we broke down and bought a big Case backhoe that cleared

Above: *Dennis the pilot. Photo courtesy of the author.*

the way to an acre of high ground—it turned out that Collins Creek split and encircled the high center like a moat.

When we learned the flood zone required us to build up 3 ½ feet, the amateur draftsman in me was confounded. Because we were in the middle of a forest, I envisioned two stories to gain a long vista over the canopy and out to the pasture and fields beyond, but I didn't want a large house. The plan I had drawn was small, but ridiculously tall.

Our dear friend Scot Zimmerman, an architectural photographer, spent many evenings in our cinderblock burrow. Witnessing my frustration, he introduced us to a client of his. We met Arthur Dyson in his office on P Street in Fresno in the old Ice House building.

Above: Arthur Dyson's office on P Street in Fresno. Courtesy of Arthur Dyson.

For two sessions, we talked about anything but architecture. His work and his words awakened our imaginations. The planning process was unorthodox. I'll explain that planning process later, but the questions had more to do with philosophy and psychology than outright design. Two years later, in 1987, we moved into the radical organic sculpture seen on the opposite page.

The Lencioni Residence has, by now, won awards, been published in books and magazines and featured on Extreme Homes, but for us it was our first real house. While Gran's death that New Year's Eve was devastating to me, the cycle of life continues: Nicolas was born in June 1988 and Dani Evelyn (named for Gran) was born the next year. This was their home when they entered school in Centerville.

Above: Lencioni House. Photo courtesy of Scot Zimmerman.

When they reached first grade, brother and sister were still sharing a loft bedroom, and every attempt to add on seemed, to me, to upset the form and balance of the house, so we moved across the road to Gran's, a well-made, custom one-story ranch house with an enclosed kitchen, a formal dining room and three bedrooms branching off a long hallway. I always intended to move back to the Creek House when the children were grown; I planned to grow old in that thrilling organic space we'd built, but I knew I'd have to wait more than a decade.

Accustomed to an open floor plan, we de-walled the Ranch House with the help of Boback Emad, now a large-form sculptor, who had apprenticed with both Dyson and John Lautner, and who had assisted Dennis on the metal details of our first house.

Above: Model of the Ranch House remodel by Dyson and Associates.
Photo courtesy of the author.

In the late '90s, we wanted to expand the living room and reorient the entry. We consulted Dyson (then dean at Taliesin), and his office presented plans that involved lifting the roof and angling it to match the 37-degree angle in the yard. Sadly, the bids came in consistently four times over our budget, and Dennis sort of stomped away from the project. My ability to render an elevation had improved, and ultimately a handyman executed the remodel based on my hand drawings. I never felt good about that exchange because I couldn't un-ring the bell of one Dysonian angle, and I recognize how wonderful Dyson's proposed design would have been, with its multiple clerestories, a sheltering overhang on the courtyard, and a glass-on-glass corner celebrating the long vista. I still have the cardboard model.

Sometime around 9/11, tragedy struck our house too as we learned that Dennis had contracted an inoperable brain tumor, and he died during the kids' freshman year at University High School in Fresno (before the

Dyson design of UHS commenced). When Art and Audrey Dyson came for Dennis' memorial service, I had too many other things on my mind to notice what they thought of my amateur design.

I married Greg Lapp, a musician, right before the children's senior year, and we all lived in the Ranch House that last year until the kids moved away to college.

All this time, I'd been renting out the first Dyson house, the Lencioni Residence, which we call the Creek House. So, with the nest suddenly empty, I sold the ranch, and Greg and I moved into the smaller Creek House as I had always intended—with Greg's full-sized Steinway.

As much as Greg loves the Creek House and appreciates the sublime organic architecture and its impact on its inhabitants, there was no getting around the fact that I had built it with Dennis. And, while Greg and I were used to cooking together, the Creek House kitchen is a one-chef space. Plus, his grand piano took up the entire dining area and part of the living room, crowding the entire downstairs. While we were used to having concerts for 50 in the Ranch House, a maximum of 21 people could squeeze into the Creek House if some perched on the staircase. We didn't want more space, but we needed our space differently configured.

I agreed, in theory, to moving, but I said it had to be as lovely as the Creek House, near water, and not too far from the college where I taught, which essentially limited us to the Kings River valley. We looked at the few houses for sale, but I felt claustrophobic in any we toured. No riverside lots were available for over a year.

One day in 2006, Greg and I were kayaking, and we spied the back side of a For Sale sign on a lot with a grass lawn that came down to the Kings River. We pulled the kayaks up, stepped off the middle part of the property to measure it, memorized the phone number on the sign, paddled quickly down to our car and phones, met the realtor an hour later (still in our water shoes). We made an offer before the end of the day.

Above: Lapp RiverHouse. Photo courtesy of the author.

Partly because of the remodel fiasco years ago on the Ranch House, we went to Art with our joint floor plan. It wasn't cheap, but it wasn't outrageous; as teachers, we are only *token* patrons of the arts. Still, the Lapp RiverHouse has already garnered two pretty significant architectural awards and is featured in magazines and a forthcoming book (besides this one). The highlights of the planning and building process are detailed in later chapters, but it was a six-year process. It's taken even longer to settle down and complete this book, which has transformed and gone back to the drawing board many times as well.

In this book, I share stories of some Dyson clients and like-minded architects I've come to know. A working title for this book was "Living in Art('s) Work: Why Organic Architecture Is Worth It," and at one point, my focus was more biographical. My examples consist primarily from the portfolio of Arthur Dyson because I've been fortunate to know many clients, apprentices, and associates of Dyson, and, of course, both my homes are his work. The professional photographs are the stunning work of my life- long friend, architectural photographer Scot Zimmerman; the amateur photos are moments I have captured; otherwise, I've labeled the source. As I attempt to describe what it's like to live in each of these houses, how each came to be, and what I have learned from the process, the project has evolved into an apologia for *all* authentic architecture— designs by all artist-architects who *get* how important it is that our dwellings reflect our *selves*.

There are aspects of our choices that are personal, obviously, and we (Dennis and I, Greg and I) have made many compromises in the name of cost, but as I show the house to more and more people, I see that the notion of *how to choose* is eminently worthy and, although people's ideas of beauty differ, the pursuit of what we each find beautiful reflects us and our values and offers us, what Gaston Bachelard calls "felicitous space." We've spent the COVID-19 pandemic quarantined here and have remained peaceful, productive, and, I venture to say, felicitous. ■

CHAPTER ONE:
ARCHITECTURE THAT DEFIES
A LABEL: OUTSIDE ANY BOX

Above: Terrace at Lapp RiverHouse.
Photo by David Swann.

"However you see them, categories are never impartial. That's not to say they're bad. But they're not neutral. They complicate rather than clarify."

—Ben Pfeiffer,
Paris Review, referring to categorizing Native American literature

With outside-the-box design, people sometimes struggle to cram the idea back into some sort of container—yet, this architecture resists a label, which presents a quandary for titling this book—what style am I actually advocating?

Dyson adamantly defies labeling his work. He says that, traditionally, many architects or architectural scholars force designs into categories, but this tendency "just creates walls and separates us." Fay Jones, another student of Frank Lloyd Wright and Bruce Goff, calls his University of Arkansas Press book *Outside the Pale*. In the introduction, Robert Adams Ivy Jr. writes that Jones' organic architecture "begins in order and ends in mystery."

Both of my houses fit pretty snugly into the "organic" category, as Dyson designed them from the inside out to accommodate views or cross-breezes, to interact with the landscape, integrate the home into its surroundings, and to respond organically to our personalities and lifestyle. Even Dyson's sharply angled designs emerge organically from an authentic source in different ways, often to capture a specific view. Of Dyson's Barrett-Tuxford Residence, owner Will Green explains: "Our house has its roots in Prairie Style architecture, but Dyson took a more organic and metaphysical path, the more difficult and risky path, to be sure." Green writes that it feels like "what Virginia Woolf called 'a moment of being.'"

To William Gray Purcell biographer Mark Hammons' mind, "reflective" is appropriate, as it reflects the setting or emerges organically from it, as it reflects and emerges organically from the personalities of the clients, and reflects what architectural writer Ann Zimmerman calls the "life rhythms" of the clients: "[Dyson] personalizes each design to the natural setting and to the life rhythms of the clients."

Giuliano Chelazzi, Italian architect and head of the Amici di Frank Lloyd Wright in Italy, in a European book about Dyson's work, calls it "meditative": *L'Archittetura Meditiva*. Chelazzi quotes architect Bruno Zevi, who describes Dyson as an "authentic architect, an animated voice that spreads optimism, a rare outburst in a world suffocated by frustration, by indifference and cynicism, by eclecticism and by rhetoric and grayness." I like the term "authentic architecture," but will it stick? As a scholar, Chelazzi is analyzing the source and inspiration for this universal organic idea, but he claims that other Italian scholars took Zevi's words and Dyson's work as "a provocation," similar to the way they disparaged Frank Lloyd Wright's Masieri Memorial project in Venice.

Chelazzi mollifies this conflict with a quote from architect Renzo Piano, who writes, "[M]y desire to explore unbeaten paths is in perfect accord with my gratitude to tradition....Certainly it is the inheritance of a humanist culture." "Humanist" architecture is another option.

In his website, *The Post-Usonian Project*, Matt Taylor features the Creek House as Post-Usonian example. Taylor focuses on the marriage of style and value, in the tradition of Wright's Usonian mission. He's worried about obsolescence and concerned that society will lose authentic design and lifestyle. Taylor writes:

> *A dedication to building an environment based on a singular view of human lifestyle: simple, uncomplicated, natural, eloquent, affordable. These are not "trophy" houses, which is why they are so vulnerable today....Their basis was [still is] a notion of lifestyle that stands, today, in sharp contrast to an over-consumptive and compulsive culture.*

Putting it in a chronological perspective, Taylor suggests:

> *In the '60s and '70s, there were several attempts to revive this [Post-Usonian] movement, mostly driven by ecological, energy, and related issues.*

Above: Lencioni Creek House awning.
Photo Courtesy of the author.

Unfortunately, the affluence of the '80s and '90s has not been generally kind to the American landscape....I used to go and visit these houses and wonder— I still wonder: what sparked their creation, what allowed the majority of work to go another way despite their enduring popularity to this day?

Perhaps "natural architecture" describes the work. It's become common to call expressive designs adapted from and inspired by biological organisms and forms "biophilic." For example, in "Architectural Lessons from Environmental Psychology: The Case of Biophilic Architecture" (2006), Yannick Joye argues for the multiple benefits of "nature-based" design in reducing stress and connecting us to our best selves, another proponent, in a slide presentation entitled "Using Less, Living More, and Being Natural," suggests "vernacular architecture was innately organic based on natural form, structure, and simple local materials." The architecture I advocate transcends the vernacular; or rather, it *promotes* a vernacular response to the landscape. A while back, Amazon, in its omniscient wisdom, suggested for me a book titled *In Search of Natural Architecture* by David Pearson.

When the book arrived, I started reading it from the back (a habit from reading architectural magazines, where the subjects I'm interested in are usually towards the end). I stopped at the Prince Residence, Corona Del Mar (p. 69) in the section on "Healing Architecture" and passed it over to Greg. "Look," I said, "the shingle pattern's like the Creek House." He started flipping pages from the front. "Did you see this?" he asked casually. In the introduction, on page 25, just before the first chapter on "Ancestral Archetypes," is a photo of our house. The text reads:

> *Since he set up practice in Fresno, in 1969, [Arthur Dyson] has produced a cascade of novel and sophisticated designs. He prefers to describe his work as "reflexive" rather than "organic" as its focus is to try to understand and express the flux of life and its myriad relationships. According to Dyson, the resulting architecture is not only practical in terms of economy and environment, but possesses the vital spark of originality that integrates and exalts the worth of the individual within the surging field of life. The building is an interactive membrane between the dynamic forces seeking expression from within and those coming from outside.*
>
> *One of his most successful designs for a private house is the Lencioni Residence [the Creek House], completed in 1986 [sic—actually, 1988] and situated in*

a forested glade in Sanger, California. It was the rhythm of the site together with the adventurous ideas of the young clients that helped Dyson to create the design's dramatic sinuous and fluid forms.

I ultimately decided that the only term whose tent covers all I want to advance is "authentic" because it includes every style that is honest, that is sincere. As Frank Lloyd Wright expresses in "Idea and Essence" (1958):

Every idea that is a true idea has a form, and is capable of many forms. The variety of forms of which it is capable determines the value of the idea. So by way of ideas, and your mastery of them in relation to what you are doing, will come your value as an architect to your society and future. That's where you go to school. You can't get it in a university…you can't get it anywhere except as you love it, love the feeling of it, desire and pursue it. And it doesn't come when you are very young, I think. I believe it comes faster with each experience, and the next is very simple, or more simple, until it becomes quite natural to you to become master of the idea you would express.

Whatever label we come up with, we're talking about artistic architecture. Because they already "get it," artists may conclude they can skip the architect and design for themselves, as I attempted with the Ranch House remodel. Recently, an artist I know asked to come see both the Creek House and the RiverHouse. He'd been in the spaces socially, but he was planning on designing and building a home/studio/gallery himself in another part of the country. Like us, he subscribes to the notion of a small, green-built house close to nature, and he was drawn to the details in an artistic home like ours. He is, as we were, on a budget. The artist thought, as I originally had, that he could hand his artistic design to a structural engineer to get through plan-check and go from there. I found myself trying to articulate my warrants to him, advocating not just for reflective, authentic design (which he was already on board with), but also for collaborating with an artist-architect, who can help him realize his complete vision.

I laid out for my artist friend:

A. Designing for your unique and overlapping workspace, social space, display space, and all the while an inspiration for an artist, requires much more skill than tastefully arranging rectangles filled with cool furniture and artwork.

B. While you are inspired by ideas that are fresh and original and appreciate creative solutions to even small problems, like me, your experience in architectural problem-solving is limited. Connecting this angle to that one with attention to the way we move through the space is complicated. Most artists deal in fewer dimensions and fewer regulations and restraints than architects.

C. As a photographer, you are sensitive to space, light, texture, sound, and color, but it takes experience to know how to maximize them in built space. Some amateurs take a great photo by chance, but a professional photographer has more experience, more techniques and understanding of the materials and, when it's done well, the result can be breathtaking.

D. Like us, you have financial limits and priorities that will mean you skimp on some things and splurge on others, but it's not just a matter of initial cost. You will undoubtedly consider energy efficiency and your time and set the priorities, but allow someone with comprehensive experience to show you the options. Just as you can pay an accountant to save you money on your taxes, an architect may reduce your costs with clever choices.

Thankfully, my photographer friend is seeking out an artist-architect in his new locale. ∎

CHAPTER TWO:
HOUSE AS REFLECTION OF OUR SELVES AND OUR ASPIRATIONS

Above: View from the upstairs bedroom at the Creek House.
Photo by Scot Zimmerman.

"It is never too late to be what you might have been"

—George Eliot,
Middlemarch

T he space you choose to inhabit is an expression of your style, values, aspirations, and self-image. It seems to me, sadly, that most houses aspire to be more ordinary than the extraordinary people inside them, an idea I'm sure originated from Art Dyson.

Architectural apathy, choosing *not* to consciously choose the fundamental design of your house, is also a decision. If you care about space, as I do, the choice is important. What you wear, what you eat, what you drive, where you vacation all express your style and your priorities. You have to eat; you have to live somewhere. Careless choices in food can have adverse health consequences; architectural fast food can likewise make you sick. Abdicating choice of dress for a uniform may inadvertently suppress your individuality.

Dyson makes the point that "nature employs the wonder of variety" and suggests architecture ought to follow suit. "Variety pleasures the soul," he says, "while uniformity suffocates it." Impression *is* important: we pick up cues about people's priorities, values, and personalities from the clothes they wear and the spaces they choose to inhabit.

It goes without saying that creative people customize homes once built for others, just as creative people find ways to express their style despite a dress code. I've been impressed by my family, friends, Art Dyson himself, making alterations to mature homes, imbuing them with their own personalities. I submit, though, that renovation, as we did with the Ranch House, is trickier and, in my experience, more costly than designing from the ground up.

Your style will reflect *your* personality, and while our choices will be different, when they are *sincere*, our lives are mostly in balance. Greg's and my style is spare, a blank canvas for nature and new ideas. Guests (and the unique styles they bring with them) contribute to the color and ornamentation of the moment. The windows are canvases framing outdoor color and movement. With its high windows, high ceilings, and glass above the interior walls, the RiverHouse reflects our generally open, guileless personalities. We want to live outside or close to it, so the indoors and outdoors feather into one another, and the illusion keeps us from feeling hemmed in. "The best modern architecture," philosopher Alain de Botton argues, "doesn't hold a mirror up to nature, though it may borrow a pleasing shape or expressive line from nature's copybook. It gives voice to aspirations and suggests possibilities." Expression of style is critical for identity, and architecture is arguably the most omnipresent and permanent opportunity for expression. I remember when my children were teenagers developing their personal style. It amused me how opposite two close siblings could be. I won't go into hairstyles and fashion choices of my own kids. Think of yours instead, or of yourself as you were developing your style.

Sometimes it makes sense to fit in. Conformity has the advantage of predictability, familiarity, efficiency. Some people don't want to make choices or just don't care; a uniform makes sense for them. Some people choose understated design so as not to stand out or to *avoid* expression. My parents designed a lovely home in Pasadena with an intentionally quiet façade; all its style is interior and directed onto a center courtyard.

Sanghita, who is from southern India, was dressing me for a Bollywood party from her three color-crowded closets of traditional dresses. She chose for me a bright pink sari with emerald accents and lots of silver and bangles and bindi. She said one adjustment of living in this country has been having to suppress her color preferences when she's in "mixed company." Her home palette is a classy muted taupe in stark contrast to the contents of her closets. While color *seems* integral to Sanghita's personality and style, she says she feels more comfortable conforming "for now." The other extreme, of course, is an in-your-face garish style in fashion or architecture. As with the complicated piercings or revealing styles of my students or people on the street—which leave me unsure whether I'm supposed to look away or if they are daring me to stare— some architecture is likewise unpleasantly and randomly weird.

When people choose architecture or architectural style simply to impress, disjointed from their personality or culture, or even era, everything seems false and out of balance. Terri Zumwalt, Dyson client and realtor, said she is astonished over and over again that people are willing to spend a fortune to build a house that's exactly like their neighbors'. "They've picked different granite, so they think they've made it their own," she says. "People aren't willing to go out on a limb because they crave affirmation and approval from other people."

I think people are afraid to authentically express themselves with architecture *because* it is such a major expense, and realtors warn about resale value to a generic buyer, who is imagined lacking any personality or style. It's as if they all got together and said: "If we make houses all the same, buyers can just exchange the old shelter for a new shelter that fits better," as if homebuyers were hermit crabs. Or, "now they have more money, so they can have the same house, only larger." It would be like saying, "now you can afford more food, so just eat more of it," which unfortunately also happens. It takes rare confidence to resist advice from a realtor, contractor, or "expert" who has little personal stake in the place in which you will sow your dreams.

Built space is not simply shelter. Most people live indoors and take for granted the form of the doors and walls and windows that surround them. They fill a house with things they find beautiful, hang beautiful art on the walls, but sometimes overlook the way we move in a space and the way space moves us. Sometimes decoration compensates effectively for pedestrian or stifling architecture, but it's a slide show compared to a movie, or a movie compared to a living, breathing live theatrical experience. For *Journal of the Taliesin Fellows*, edited by Michael Hawker, I wrote "Surrounded by Sculpture: The Joy and Value of Organic Architecture" (October 2011)—here's an excerpt in which I try to capture the movement:

> *I just turned off the lights in the house to let the moon in. While I type at the kitchen bar, the half moon shines insistently through the highest windows at the top of the arched ceiling. Even as October clouds veil its intensity, that moon shines a path across the living room table, and the cool night air settles like a clean sheet.*

If an architect's designs are customized for each client—as Dyson says, "the appearance of the work is a product of the individual uniqueness of the clients...[intended] to fulfill their potential to live and work in the most meaningful way," what impact does the space have on a second owner or someone who rents? Certainly hermit crabs situate themselves into another organic space that was created for another creature; but we are not crabs, or as psychologically malleable. Some renters have felt uneasy with the open format and the lack of wall space or privacy in my homes, but some have flourished in this space. When we moved to the Ranch House, my dear friend Kristine Walter moved into the Creek House, making a clean break from various entanglements. I asked Kris what it was like for her to live in a house designed for me. She said she appreciated the way the small living room expands as it merges with the deck. "Upstairs is astonishing; it's like living in a tree house." She remembered the play of light and shadow, calling it "meditative, almost sacred." It was a good place for her to regroup and poise herself for a conscious refocusing of her life. Kris's daughter Sarah, visiting when she was in her twenties, said she mostly remembers the setting tucked in the forest. "I loved that I felt totally outside, even when I was inside," she said. "Because the architecture is so unique, we could play explorer in the house." Even though Sarah was only a second-grader at the time, she is aware on another level how important the move was for reasons unrelated to architecture (but possibly soothed by it). "It was time for doing something different," Sarah said. "And it was different; maybe since the house was so unlike our old one, that helped—it was a risk [to quit a job, move, remarry], but moving into that house was my mom's first step for happiness."

Personality and style matter; site and the surroundings matter; but so does the historical time period. The more personal a design, the less bound it is to its birthdate. In the 1990s, the Creek House won Sunset's award for a house 10 years old. In its singularity, the design is timeless. I admire buildings built in every decade, every century, and it's worth preserving the best examples of all architecture. Some of it can be creatively renovated or up-cycled. We visited Greg's friends in Belgium who converted a stone stable from the 1700s into a lovely modern home reflecting their innovative personalities. But if I'm building from scratch today in America, I'm building a contemporary American home, not a Tudor. I love to read and teach Shakespeare, but I don't write in the same English as the Bard (forsooth), nor do I dress in Elizabethan fashion. "Architecture has joined the world of fashion, but fashion is passing and architecture is timeless," says Israeli architect Moshe Safdie. I subscribe to this notion as long as the architecture is authentic and reflects the personality of the clients, not the trends of the times. Dyson explained, in a 2014 interview with an architecture student that a problem in architecture education is the tendency to teach from the past, rather than imagine for the future.

> I thoroughly understand that for many, a return to the past is comforting. But for me a meaningful architecture should be a beautiful refuge, an emotional structure, not a frozen piece of history. I see "traditional" architecture as appearing more concerned with honoring the dead than the living.

Commenting on a letter to the editor of The Fresno Bee (January 16, 2005) on the proposed design for the late Fresno Metropolitan Museum, Dyson questions the letter-writer's desire to "incorporat[e] the architectural styles from the surrounding area" to "reflect the neo-Renaissance style" of adjacent buildings. Dyson counters that such a move would create nothing but "more copies of another time and place." The letter-writer fears, "the futuristic architectural style of the proposed museum expansion will clash horribly with downtown Fresno." The writer, James A. Sigala, contends:

> Fresno's insecurity complex is revealed with the history of its downtown— never content with oneself—always tearing down the past and replacing it with new modern identities (buildings). Do the giant birdcage from the 1960s, also known as the Fresno County Courthouse, or the spaceship design of Fresno's City Hall ring a bell?

Art agrees that architecture reflects its community. "However," he writes in his response, "Fresno has the opportunity to speak with its own voice, expressing the pride and confidence of its citizenry, just as the Renaissance architects did in their time....A culture is not created by pilfering images from the past, but by conceiving its own authentic vision." Those reticent to change rely heavily on the word, "complement," as if the word means "replicate." Sigala's letter concludes: "Downtown Fresno's true rebirth will commence only when future buildings are designed to complement it, instead of challenging the downtown with odd and contemporary architecture."

What is new is always suspect, but there have to be new ideas or we languish.

Harvey Ferrero tells a story about the Bruce Goff–designed Ruth Ford House in Aurora, Illinois, "back in '45 or so," with an exterior of coal. "He did a couple houses like that. It was a hard coal from Pennsylvania that was laid up like masonry." Ferrero narrates the scene:

> The woman across the street came over and said, "What is that house made of?" and Bruce Goff said, "It's made of coal." And she said, "Well, won't

that burn?" to which Goff responded, "Where do you live?"

"I live right there across the street."

"In that wooden house?"

"Yes."

"Well, won't that burn?"

Eric Lloyd Wright emphasized, "My grandfather was very harsh on imitation. He said, 'If you really understand what I'm talking about—the principles—then you'll be creating your own forms. They will be coming out of those principles of mine, but they won't be imitating my work. They'll be your essence, and your character will be expressed in the building.'"

So architecture produces our environment, our human habitat, and many people (not just the über-wealthy) can choose to create a space that is stimulating or soothing. "One of the great, but often unmentioned, causes of both happiness and misery," writes de Botton, "is the quality of our environment: the kind of walls, chairs, buildings and streets we're surrounded by. And yet a concern for architecture and design is too often described as frivolous, even self-indulgent." In *The Architecture of Happiness*, de Botton suggests: "where we are heavily influences what we can be...it is architecture's task to stand as an eloquent reminder of our full potential." Writer Mark Hammons says architecture has the potential to shake us from our persistent torpor. "People need to wake up," he insists, "and the single most profoundly powerful force that governs your waking, sleeping, and every moment in between is architecture. The choices that you make versus the choices that you allow other people to make—or those which you must endure—are entirely up to you." He sets his hands on the table in his Los Angeles garden apartment and leans forward. "You can resign yourself to a strip mall existence if you want." He points to the shops crowded into a parking lot at the end of his street.

T.C. Boyle ✓
@tcboyle

🔸 **Follow** ∨

The elfin cottage where K. & I will stay tonight.

Above: Tweet by T.C. Boyle, who came to read at Reedley College.
Photo courtesy of the author.

"You can pretend to be Lord or Lady *Whatever* if you want. But if instead you wish to encounter the *substance of life,* if you wish to engage your spiritual evolution as a human being in the here and now, this [the design of your surroundings] is something you need to consider."

Who would dislike this architecture? Hammons writes: "Sometimes rejection is dressed courteously in remarks about artistic eccentricity, implying an untrustworthy frivolity or strangeness of character." Direct scoffing, he writes, results from "virgin ignorance." My first house has often been referred to as a sculpture, usually in a positive way, but even people close to me have remarked, "I don't think it's necessary to live in a sculpture." Reactions to the Creek House have ranged from awe to amusement to disdain. On the website *Architizer*, a forum for architectural discussion, comments about the Creek House range from descriptive, "like poetry frozen in wood and glass"; to comical, "Hobbit's nest" and *"que pena…Frodo Bolsón debe de estar de viaje, no se le ve en la foto de su casa"* (which, by my rude translation, says, "Silly Frodo must be on a journey because he's not in the picture of his house"); to flattering, "magnificent" and "so beautiful"; to flaming, "holy s**t. tell me this is a joke."

A house reflects the occupants' aspirations, and we have aspired to bring culture to country living (think *Middlemarch*) and to draw family and friends to our remote location. To that end, we offer hospitality, the view, and a relaxing, pleasing, even inspirational style. I do think it's a community service to build beautiful architecture, but we don't aspire to vapid grandeur. Reflecting the Sierra foothills as the RiverHouse does, hugging the hillside and flowing like the river beside it, the home harmonizes with the landscape. Harmony—we aspire to harmony. ∎

CHAPTER THREE: ARCHITHERAPY: HOW ARCHITECTURE IMPACTS OUR LIVES AND WELL-BEING

Above: *Lapp RiverHouse interior.*
Photo by David Swann.

"First we shape our buildings, then they shape us."

—Winston Churchill

have thought a lot about the psychological impact of space and how the space we inhabit affects the way we feel and act. I call this architherapy. From Barbara Harwood's *The Healing House*, I learned that Churchill delivered his comment about architherapy (above) twice, once when addressing the English Architectural Association in 1924, and again to advocate the rebuilding of Parliament in 1943. I view the statesman's words as cautionary: beware of how we shape our buildings, lest they shape us in unintended ways. Politically speaking, we live in a society that is increasingly stratified: ostentatious estates and gated tract-mansions stand in stark contrast to tract-shacks and mobile homes. It's possible the disparity will lead to pitchforks. The loneliness of the one sharply contrasts the overcrowded conditions of the other. In the news, we see a suburban couple armed, pointing weapons at peaceful protesters marching by. "Communities" are rigidly homogeneous, and the result is utter misunderstanding and mistrust between the different groups of people. Houses designed for an income-based stratum ignore the individual personalities of people within that group—at society's peril. I like to drive through older modest neighborhoods, where the designs, while not *notable*, often present interesting and particular choices, and each house has an earnest personality. It's heartening to see neighborhoods like these across the country rejuvenating and translating the individuality and aspirations of the new owners into architectural renewal, so the architecture can support and nourish them in return.

To successfully achieve form, architecture as inhabited art must reflect the specific kilter of the minds of those who live there. By subjecting people to controlled environments, Dyson says, you can control, to a certain extent, their whole attitude both psychologically and physiologically. You can raise their blood pressure, you can lower it—you can control a whole wide range of things. "You need to know how these things work to begin with, and then you need to intuit how your clients are going to respond." It only makes sense that a home should instill peace, stability, and just the right amount of stimulation. On a summer day, a friend called to tell me her husband was seriously ill. Rather than talk on the phone, she drove up the hill and, in this peaceful space, we talked about the options, issues, and everything else, and she left calmer and fortified. When my artist daughter faced a stressful episode in her life, she flew from New York City for "RiverHouse therapy."

Greg and I feel soothed and well in our house; at the same time, the glass and light and curve and shadow energize us. Musician and Dyson client Bill Kelly says he feels more creative in his home—he's easily over-stimulated if there's too much going on in a room, if there's too much clutter. Kelly's son Kevin, who is high-functioning autistic, thrives in his home, he says. In an over-stimulating environment, Kevin can become agitated or act out, Kelly said, but "when he's at this house, he is noticeably more calm than when he's elsewhere." Kevin came in the room while we were talking and sat down as calmly as his father had testified. He sat back in his chair and listened for a while before he went on to do something else.

For me, there's the problem of the square: when I must work in a close rectilinear space, I subconsciously cock my chair at an angle. I'll feel nervous and a little trapped. Heidi Julavits, in *The Folded Clock*, catalogues rooms that lack escape options or have too many unprotected entrances (obviously problems for different types of people). She wonders if "people mistook for ghost sightings what was, in fact, a primal fear response to poorly arranged rooms." My office at the college, for instance, has a fixed window facing the blank side of the Forestry building ("lack of escape options") and on the opposite side a narrow glass panel (that some professors *cover up!*) and a solid door, which I (with apologies to my dear colleagues) never close and face when I'm not glued to the computer. "Do you want me to close the door, Mrs. Lapp?" students ask as they leave. It's all I can do not to fling myself at the door to keep it from shutting. I feel I need "room" to think. In an essay from her book *Thin Places* called "The Big Empty," Jordan Kisner illustrates this point:

> *Saying I can't get enough space is just another way of saying that I'm not thinking very well and that this problem of thinking feels at least partially spatial. If you conceive of the mind as a thing that has dimensionality, something that when you close your eyes seems to stretch up and out and behind and beyond you, then it is easy to imagine the mind as a place that one can move about in...*

> *Which suggests, possibly, that if you are stuck somewhere small in your mind, somewhere unhappy or afraid or paralyzed or heartbroken, all of which are a kind of claustrophobic circling and circling, you might be able to reverse engineer an expansion, shove yourself through into some larger mind place by putting yourself in the way of some vaster spaces in the world.*

Your home shouldn't confine you, but free you to be as authentically yourself as possible. Extolling the psychological benefits of organic architecture, David Pearson writes in *New Organic Architecture*:

> *Emphasizing beauty and harmony, [organic architecture's] free-flowing curves and expressive forms are sympathetic to the human body, mind, and spirit. In a well-designed "organic" building, we feel better and freer.*

I notice that we borrow expressions from rectilinear architecture, such as "boxed in" and "cornered" to express a desperate sort of constraint. Architecturally, too many boxed-in corners limit our freedom. Writing in *L'Architettura*, architect Karl Ashley Smith suggests of Arthur Dyson's work: "[Dyson's architecture] has captured a constituent element of the American spirit: the contradictory desire of being rooted, settled into the land, and yet to be free to roam the vastness of the frontiers, to be ever exploring, growing, and changing." Dyson client Tom Jaksha compares inhabiting a rectilinear house, which is designed to protect a person *from* nature, to inhabiting a Dyson or Mickey Muennig Home, which flows with nature's rhythms—"with the harmony between man and nature. It's like saying, 'I'm back to where I'm supposed to be.'" He extols their Sumner Hill house as "aggressively reaching out to nature."

I think it has to do with balance. In every part of life, we hope to achieve balance: in our diets, our work-play dynamic, the yin and yang of our relationships, give and take. Greg will feel overly busy at work with concerts and touring gigs and looming AP tests his students hope to pass, but by the time I hear the gate open, he has plugged in his car, slung his briefcase on the counter just inside the door, and I see him physically adjust his posture, sigh deeply, and smile. "Few of us are entirely well balanced," writes Alain de Botton and John Armstrong in *Art as Therapy*. So many different factors in our attitudes and daily routines send our emotions inclining, "grievously in one direction or another." The philosopher and art historian diagnose a series of extremes you may recognize: "We may, for example, have a tendency to be too complacent, or too insecure; too trusting, or too suspicious; too serious, or too light-hearted." They contend, "[A]rt [and, I would say, architecture in particular] can put us in touch with concentrated doses of our missing dispositions, and thereby restore a measure of equilibrium to our listing inner selves."

Every person's psychology has different spatial requirements, and working closely with an artist-architect can result in the right configuration for your own mind. As de Botton points out, "[W]e are not all missing the same things." Pairing a photo of a Ludwig Mies van der Rohe, sleek, wood-paneled room with a white rug and glass walls protected by oak trees ("a home to rebalance the nervous soul") with a rococo Mexican cathedral ("art to rebalance a Norwegian civil servant"), he concludes, "[T]he art that has the capacity to rebalance us, and therefore arouse our enthusiasm, will differ markedly." He writes that the last thing a person in a boring job needs is the symmetry and order of Mies van der Rohe.

Incidentally, Dyson told me, "van der Rohe's personal apartment was furnished with overstuffed chairs, not the modern Barcelona chairs one would expect." For the cubical worker, de Botton and Armstrong prescribe instead, "Flamenco music, the paintings of Frieda Kahlo and the architecture of [Taxco] Mexico's Catedral de Santa Prisca—varieties of art that might help restore life to our slumbering souls." In the RiverHouse, we love the wall of windows, but *you* may feel exposed; one neighbor shifted her eyes nervously and called it a "fishbowl." You may prefer snug little rooms (you'd prefer to sleep, then, in our den). You might feel enlivened with all your stuff on display, while clutter makes me uncomfortable. I lived for a short time in a travel trailer by the river, tight as a pocket. Fortunately, common picnic tables, laundry area, and the river made it livable; I slipped myself inside my pocket-closet only to sleep. Similarly, I only slept in my basement room in a house in San Francisco, a vast rectangle with windows well above my head—my view was my housemates' ankles and the neighbors' cats—and I spent my waking and working hours by the wraparound kitchen window.

Architecture elicits a soulful response and, as such, has the power to harm or heal. In the Creek House, the sun enters in panels of light on the floor through windows of all different shapes with precious few right angles. Light in the RiverHouse likewise refracts just as music from the piano resonates along the curved ceiling and wall. As musicians and brain scientists claim about the "Mozart Effect," in which spatial-temporal reasoning is heightened by listening to layered music, this complex and flowing architecture stimulates my brain. When I asked architect Larry Brink about architecture's ability to heal, he said, "I think the right kind of architecture can be very therapeutic because we're taught to use all the natural surroundings—the sun, the light, the natural way of bringing nature in the house." He remarked that, as the sun creates different patterns throughout the day, "it's a different house; it changes moods during the day. I think these happenings help people." The play of light, he said, nudges the brain to work in different ways, "to create the space which Mr. Wright called 'having spirit.' It's not something that just sits there, it's a living work of art." Dyson says, "Humans are fascinating and complicated beings, and it is my solemn belief that architecture can substantially and meaningfully improve their condition and uplift their spirits." Roseanne Guaglione, a designer who worked with Dyson on the Interior Systems remodel, said in an interview, "I really believe that interior spaces can edify or agitate someone's spirit, and [Dyson] just seems to be in tune with and honoring of the Earth." Her building is dynamic, made of metal and glass and concrete, but Guaglione said, "Even though there are angles and glass divided in shards, the windows still have a very organic feeling to them, and you can see the sky where most places this small don't allow you to see sky." She said, "There was the most beautiful softness to that space when you walked inside. The building was inviting and had a whimsical, almost a cartoon-like invitation to it. When you got inside, those raw floors, the softness of the wall color, and the way the walls were canted out, it just was very room-like and enveloping, and it felt really good to be in there."

Color, texture, and sound impact us in the same way light and shadow do; so, if our choices reflect our needs and intention rather than fashion or custom, we'll be more satisfied. "For most people, color has an enormous importance in the experience of architecture," says Dyson. "Personal surroundings reflect emotional patterns and tendencies through the presence of hue, tone, and shade across the visible spectrum of light." I describe his intent, in the planning questionnaire, to discern a client's response to color and sound (he correlates the two). He says fast food restaurants' interior orange urges customers to eat quickly, get up and go (for quick turnaround). In the early grief of widowhood, I painted my bedroom walls a burnt orange to nudge myself out of bed. A friend painted her dining room a stunning and stylish "merlot," but it tended to make me sleepier than the dinner wine warranted. When I asked Eric

Wright about the effect architecture has on people's psyches, his answer mostly dealt with color and texture.

Wright said he'd discussed color with Art (Dyson's research at the San Francisco Institute of Architecture was on the psychological effects of color). "I myself tend more towards earth tones. I *like* black and white, but in a room I think it's deadly. If a client wants it light, I'll go with more of an off-white." In the Creek House, I chose a blue-infused white as a cool balance to so much wood. I chose a warmer white to balance the steel and grays in the RiverHouse. Wright said even the finishes on the wood affect the tenor of a room. He likes to leave the wood natural. When it was affordable, he liked to use copper and let it age naturally, or sometimes he'd even hasten the patina. With the wrong or right proportions of space and light and color, Eric Lloyd Wright said, "you could have a room that could drive you mad. Or," indicating the view of trees and the Pacific in his studio he shares with his artist wife Mary, "you could have another room that would relax and sooth; *this* [his studio] has *repose*." Dyson recently designed a residential crisis center in Fresno implementing all these principles. "It had to be fresh, clean, and organized, as well as safe," he said. The colors are muted grays and browns, soft and warm. The textures are varied, yet predictable—long, horizontal blocks, materials that look like natural wood, and quartz counters. Even if the residents' lives are in a state of flux, "at least the materials will be honest and natural." To make it more natural and less institutional, glass windows open up to planted areas outside, even at the ends of the hallways, and the hallways are lined with the residents' artwork. The natural light and greenery are more humanizing and hopeful, he said, pointing to the grape ivy scaling the fence outside his conference room window. "See how it waves?"

Can architecture imprint on a child? Matt Taylor spoke with Professor Hanna of the Frank Lloyd Wright's Hanna House at Stanford:

> *Professor Hanna was clearly in love with his environment, which evolved with him and Mrs. Hanna as they raised a family and built individual careers. I*

could see that it had become an integral part of their life and that living in it had deeply affected their view of life. He talked about the impact the environment had on his children as they were growing up...a magical introduction for me.

In a conversation in the Creek House, Al Struckus, a client of Bruce Goff's, proposed that children might grow up more creative in a less restrictive space such as our houses (Goff's Struckus and Dyson's Lencioni Residences), and he asked me what I thought. "Children are inherently creative," I answered. "It's society that conspires to choke them into conformity." We decided that at least the freer organic space doesn't do anything to stifle their creativity and agreed that the ready access to nature is healthy and stimulating. While I didn't think to ask about Struckus's children, my children are both creative in different ways. Marc Dyson, who grew up around his father's houses, said coexisting with these unconventional shapes gave him permission to see forms in a vast variety of ways. "More important," said Marc, "is the philosophy behind it—the way [the artist-architect/his father] solves problems—no matter what it is, he finds a creative solution." Bronwen Cohen, chief executive of *Children in Scotland,* in his 2010 "Space to Develop: How Architecture Can Play a Vital Role in Young Children's Lives," lists six premises for healthy child space:

- Offers the potential for creative play

- Encourages the children to be more naturally active

- Offers a flexible natural environment for exploring and learning

- Provides an environment where children can learn to assess risk and make informed choices

- Encourages wildlife habitation

- Has social spaces for better interaction

Architecture can influence all of these. If you grow up in a box, it's hard to think outside of that box. If the space is creative, Marc Dyson

Above: Pillars at University High School, Fresno.
Photo by Scot Zimmerman.

says, children must feel freer to explore and follow the expressive example in which they live. If windows frame wildlife and the natural environment, even in cities where the wildlife are squirrels and pigeons, children can interact with the untamed, natural world. And, while too many children are sequestered in their own little box of a room with a television or video games, children who interact with each other and with adults in a common space have more opportunity to grow socially. Eric Lloyd Wright especially espoused stimulating organic space for students in schools, dismissing suggestions he'd heard that a storefront would suffice. "You can't tell me," he said, "that the environment that surrounds those children doesn't have an impact. Especially if you're doing it in an organic way—you're bringing nature inside, and it also moves outside, so the child is engrossed and develops in the natural environment." Dyson has designed several schools, including University High School, where Greg teaches music. Greg's choir room is painted yellow and emanates energy; the room where he teaches music theory is a calmer maroon. Whimsical circles in the pillars attract students to sit, linger, and play.

At UHS and other schools and libraries, Dyson includes cozy spaces that attract children's curiosity. At the Orange Cove Children's Center, child-high windows allow children to look out and see the green and natural world outside. A skylight in the center shines on a rug and hits each month in turn, so each child's birthday month is eventually illuminated. Perhaps the most dramatic example of architecture impacting children is Dyson's design for Webster Elementary School in Fresno. In an interview, principal Elva Coronado described its impact as "a beacon of hope":

> It was designed so uniquely. There'd never been a school like this in Fresno.
>
> The children were proud of it, you know, and [as a result of the design] we didn't have the crime there. We became very good friends with the people who lived on the perimeter of the school, and they would watch the school for us on the weekends. [Dyson] would tell the parents, "This is going to be a school for your children, your families." He wanted it to be the neighborhood attraction, and it created a lot of pride in the community.

The California Standards Test (CST) scores rose 102 points the first year and 80 points the year after that, and Coronado attributed the continued improvement to the pride the teachers, the students, and the families took in the school. So that Coronado could be available to the students, Dyson designed the principal's office with windows facing the playground, the school entrance, and the library that Coronado wanted as the school's hub. In a crime-stunted area of town, the school is uniquely crime-free.

Architecture impacts behavior the way attire impacts behavior. I assume I am typical in that I dress differently for my different roles (in that way, fashion is more flexible than habitat). I have a different awareness of my surroundings depending on my costume. When students on a field trip dress up, they are on their best behavior. The same reaction occurs in built space. Alain de Botton, in *The Architecture of Happiness*, writes, "Belief in the significance of architecture is premised on the notion that we are, for better or for worse, different people in different places—and on the conviction that it is architecture's task to render vivid to us who we might ideally be."

De Botton contends buildings talk to us. Of course they do. Houses speak in the imperative, the declarative, and the interrogatory voices. The RiverHouse imperatively urges me to look up, look out at the hills, sit down, relax, appreciate. She declares: you are free, you are balanced, you are safe, you are welcome, you are part of the larger world.

She asks, "What do you want to do today?" "What do you think?" In other spaces I might eat my oatmeal standing at a counter while reading the *New York Times* online, but this house insists that I carry my breakfast back to the window, coaxing me like a good friend who knows better than I do what I need. Watching the light from various windows attempt this pose and that (and they are dazzling), often untethers a floating idea or two. Mark Hammons, in "To Architecture" (1994), writes: "Architecture can be understood as a means of providing directions, some subtle and others overt, for our behavior." Tom and Sue Jaksha tell a story of a time their Dyson home provided overt direction: Sue's parents were visiting, and they turned all the lights off and turned on "this funky contemporary jazz." Tom said the full moon cast a pattern on the floor, and they could see out to the lights of the city. "My dad was lying on the floor," Sue said, indicating how unusual that would be. "We all sort of started dancing to the music. My mom has never been drunk or high, but she started dancing as if she were. She asked, 'Is this what it's like [to be high or drunk], because that's how I feel.' It was magical." She continued. "So many people said, why do you need these cutout skylights—can't you just cover them? Art was certain that we needed them, so we agreed, and then, when I'd get up in the night, I'd sit in the moonlight under the patterns from the full moon. The house lights are out, but the city lights glow all night."

I was able to visit the Jaksha Residence with a new owner and heard similar reactions to the architecture. "When people come to the house they kind of melt," said Susan Early, who herself relaxed on a stuffed armchair with her knees tucked under her, so calm and peaceful in this space. "When people see this house for the first time, they are surprised. It's so unprepossessing from the road, then they step in and it's so *different*. Then they're surprised because it's not just another variation on the same thing, but it's unique and really *works*." Referring to the boulder in the entry, she says people are impressed it is warmer or softer than one would expect a rock to be. Chelazzi, the Italian architect and architectural scholar said, when we were discussing second owners, "while the house was not built for Early, she is very happy there." As de Botton writes, "It seems reasonable to suppose that people will possess some of the qualities of the buildings they are drawn to." Of the Jaksha Residence, Chelazzi said (translated from Italian by Dani Lencioni), "The effort was realized, I think. For a house made like this, the house and the architect are raised together.... Also the psychological, sociological, and economical dimensions— everything—are very important. But it's very important that the client makes an effort to understand that which is still incomprehensible. *Non si arrivano un succeso*. If not, they do not arrive at success." The success is manifest in the compatibility between architecture and occupant.

Anticipating need for separate space can minimize distress. The Creek House, intimate as it is, has a large and enclosed suite with a balcony for parents to retreat from teenagers' activities downstairs (and yet we could have kept an eye on them if they had been troublemakers). The office space is intentionally a private refuge. In the RiverHouse, sliding shoji- style doors have the ability to close off the den from the otherwise open space. Boback Emad told me about of one of Dyson's homes, *Vuelos de Cobre*, designed with two wings—his and hers—with a bridge connecting. Dyson designed Lela and Charles Hilton a lovely home with soft curves and a three-story glass wall, which makes the most of the Gulf view but remains private to the street. A large circular window at the entry allows light into the hallway, but the way the wall undulates away from the door, it deprives line of sight into the house. The Hilton Residence is large enough for many occupants, but they built a separate house for their adult son with special needs.

Art is proud of the glorious Hilton House, but speaks most enthusiastically about planning the healing house adjacent to the parents' for Chip. While the doctor saw Chip as a "case," Art praised the schizophrenic-bipolar man's intelligence and humor. Dyson's idea was that if he could dramatically improve a person's mental health with a home design, it would be "an amazing opportunity to offer something other folks would learn from." Dyson said he designed Chip's house to be "embracive inside and abrasive outside." Since Chip was concerned about living in such a remote setting, Art hoped he'd feel secure inside the thick stucco walls that appear fortress-like and private. While the parents' house is buoyant and light with a glass staircase exposed to the sea, Chip's house feels like a protective cape. As you look out the windows that face the Gulf of Mexico, your back and shoulders feel securely covered. The water is calm and serene. The colors are calm also, and each room monochromatic.

We hope not to be forced into the wrong architecture, but some spaces will impact us negatively. "Sensitivity to architecture also has its more problematic aspects," de Botton suggests. "If one room can alter how we feel, what will happen to us in most of the places we are forced to look at and inhabit? It is to prevent the possibility of permanent anguish that we can be led to shut our eyes to most of what is around us." I deeply desire everyone to experience his or her own best world with wide open eyes.

Architecture cannot magically dissolve all anxiety. "We should be kind enough not to blame buildings for our own failure to honour the advice they can only ever subtly proffer," says de Botton. Similarly, while many people experience a de-stressing with yoga, one yoga instructor I know who struggles with OCD freely admits yoga doesn't solve her obsessive behavior, but it does help her manage it. Alain de Botton and Armstrong call art a tool: "Like other tools, art has the power to extend our capacities beyond those that nature has originally endowed us with. Art compensates for certain inborn…psychological frailties." I can work at the RiverHouse for longer stretches than I can anywhere else, but after three hours at my computer, I must move to release the nervous demon. Unwound and reacquainted with the beauty around me, I return to work and am soothed all over again. Dyson likes to paraphrase John Lloyd Wright talking about his father's mission: "Mr. Wright designed a romance around his clients," Dyson says. "He wanted to make their sunsets brighter, make them walk with more rhythm in their step. Maybe see shadows with a paler shade of lavender." ■

CHAPTER FOUR:
CUTTING CORNERS AND COOKIE CUTTERS: REGARDING COST AND "FEASIBILITY"

Above: *Lencioni Creek House.*
Photo by Scot Zimmerman.

—Headline in *The Fresno Bee*,
Dyson home in the 1970s

W hat type of people can afford a home designed expressly for them? Fred Stitt says there's a common myth that a custom building must cost more. "You don't have to use expensive materials; it's the expression that you give the materials. It's like two painters," Stitt said. "You give one person who is a very fine painter the same brushes, the same colors, and the same canvas as another who doesn't know what he's doing. One will be a mess and one a real work of art." Dyson echoes the sentiment, saying, "Design is not a matter of cost but of composition. Like writing music, you can take inanimate notes and make them sing. Like producing a great play: you don't need lavish sets; the words work without them. A good cook can transform the most inexpensive ingredients to make a great meal." Stitt adds that sometimes the cost benefit is long-term: "Thanks to green building, mostly instigated by Frank Lloyd Wright, operating costs can be very low," not even mentioning the enduring value of a one-of-a-kind work of art.

There's the perception, often real, of increased cost with a unique design, but value isn't always tied to initial price tag. Pre-fab is cheaper, just as clothes at Walmart are cheaper, and which we consumers repeatedly buy and discard. Occupants spend money, which adds up, to half-heartedly adorn replicate houses with color spot shrubs and seasonal flags, and they stuff garages to the gills, so the cars (which are by contrast sleek and clean) rest in the short plug of a driveway. Looking down the street, you see a whole row of houses sticking out their automotive tongues. Will Green, an owner of a Dyson-designed home in Wisconsin, said, "We do have another home in California, and it is the aesthetic and spiritual equivalent of a disposable razor. I don't *mind* disposable razors, but I have to *not think* about it too much." Ours is a short-sighted and disposable culture: how many clothes in your closet go unworn or end up at Goodwill? Choosing only what is worthy, we can waste less and spend less in the long run.

A home is not an impulse buy, but an infrequent and major investment. The choice of habitat is critical, close behind career choice or choice of life partner. In this day and age, it can be almost easier to move jobs or divorce than to buy or sell a home.

When considering a design that's authentically their own, people sometimes counter: for the same money they could have twice the square feet. I ask what they would do with all those *square feet*? Too much space in a house is like too many words in a story or a song with too many verses. In *The Not So Big House*, Sarah Susanka coins the "'starter castle complex'—describing houses designed to impress rather than nurture." A doctor friend confides that his house literally gives him a stomachache. He bought it because "it seemed like the kind of house a doctor should live in," and as soon as the kids are grown he and his wife plan to find someplace that is "more them."

For us, our values in every case have featured conservation of resources, financial and environmental, and we've implemented every reasonable green innovation possible. "Innovation" implies new technology, but the "innovations" range from modern to prehistoric. We borrowed a concept from the Anasazi, for instance; we stretched a canvas awning on the Creek House to shade the southern side of the house in summer in the same way the Mesa Verde Cliff Palace in Southern Colorado protects the dug-out rooms from the higher summer sun and heat, yet welcomes in the warming winter sun. Overhangs extending 15 feet protect the RiverHouse great room from exposure in the summer.

I think it's important not to barricade myself from the elements. The house can *modify* the outside temperature, but we still experience the

Above: A cool roof and generous overhang protect from the heat.
Photo courtesy of the author.

natural fluctuation and tune our routine to the weather. From Old World and Depression-era farmers and craftsmen, we borrow cross-draft "technology" to capture the breeze off the river, and ceiling fans and whole house fan circulate the air. Dyson's Runyon Residence modulates temperature with a solar chimney. Exciting developments in new energy-efficient technologies such as radiant-floor heating and cool roofs make our commitment to green living feasible.

Sometimes it pays to wait. Greg and I waited to install solar panels, for instance, because, with the price of early solar panels and our low energy consumption, we calculated it would take 74 years to repay our investment. When the payoff came down to 16 years, we went ahead and installed the panels on our carport roof.

We are ardently thrifty and live lightly on the land. Dyson's former boss contrasted his philosophy to ours. In an interview in his Fresno office, Lee Gage said, "Art likes that sustainability—me, I just like to slap a dual pack on and be done with it." Gage predicted the future will involve fewer architects. "Art does everything custom, but I now do the work of four architects because what I do is so repetitive. Hotel plans used to be 30 pages long, now they're 90 pages, but I can do 90 pages now quicker than I could do 30. My standard of living has gone up because I produce more work, but so does my competition." He used the word "feasibility" many times in our conversation, as if feasibility precedes design and sustainability.

By contrast, Harvey Ferrero explained, "An artist-architect is probably trying to do something with the soul, more spiritual, and more poetic. Really, trying to look at it idealistically, I think the difference is the artist-architect is not a slave to the client." Ferrero added, "The regular professional architect, when the client says, 'I want a commercial structure and I want it done this way and that way,' they leave practical planning, circulation, and that sort of thing to the architect, but they want to control the overall aesthetic. And naturally, of the total utmost importance is cost, and they want it as cheap as possible. But they want it to appear as expensive as can be." Said Gage, "A lot of my clients are business clients who don't want to offend most of the people. They say, 'Give me a box, and make it look decent. If it's too far out, people won't want to do business with me because they think I'm a little eccentric or priced out of their range, so they won't come and buy my merchandise. So let's make it more plain and simple—make it feasible and get the cost down so I can

Above: The pool at the Ranch House angled toward the setting sun. Photo courtesy of the author.

build it and make some money." By contrast, he said, "People's houses are their castles. They live there every day." He laughed when I suggested people do continue to *live* in the hours they spend at work.

At the Ranch House, Emad was my ally as I insisted on accentuating the view of the oak forest by projecting the pool and cement strips at a 37-degree angle from the house (which involved moving the pasture fence). Dennis and his engineer brothers contended that a pool parallel to the house would be "just fine" (but *just fine*, I contend, is the language of settling for something, a vision only partially realized. Dennis was precise in his blacksmithing; why would "just fine" suffice when all it meant was moving a fence?). While I won that battle based on the fact that I could lifeguard the entire length of the pool from my desk if it angled that way, even the engineers in the family ultimately conceded the design was worth it. The resulting lap pool thrusts dynamically out from the window where I worked and directs your eyes to the oak forest and the southwest fingers of the setting sun. With rain or irrigation, the pool and pasture beyond appear as a dreamy river. I have a photo of Nico, age 10, standing on the vanishing edge of the pool serenading the countryside with his horn.

Several architects, when I asked about cost-saving measures, drew a direct line from their emphasis on energy efficiency back to Frank Lloyd Wright. Tours of Taliesin and Taliesin West reveal clever energy-saving techniques based on an organic lifestyle. As Minerva Montooth described in a conversation in 2017, the organic lifestyle pervades all aspects of their lives, even down to their social interactions. She suggested organic design might both nurture and reveal an organic dynamic.

By the time we built the RiverHouse, I knew enough to reduce our "budget" by 50 percent when I approached contractors, subcontractors, even my dear architect. Just as an $80K budget became a $120K reality in 1987 at the Creek House, our professed budget for the RiverHouse increased by a predictable 50 percent. In both cases, we felt the cost was worth it. I don't feel uncomfortable revealing this since my research confirms that even (or especially) the architects with the deepest aesthetic integrity have a vague concept of the actual cost of building, and the ones who focus on cost don't always challenge their clients to expand their willingness to engage their home's potential. Take-away: to reduce stress, anticipate a 50 percent increase as you plan your budget. If your ceiling is $600K, open your negotiations with a budget of $400K.

Since we're on the topic of money, this is probably a good place to mention that, when I sold them, each of the first two houses roughly quadrupled my investment, allowing me to fund the next one.

I figure there are three variables in the home construction equation: quality, cost, and time. Quality results from paying attention to details. Sidney Mukai, our contractor, was on the job every day, usually armed with a laser-level. Having apprenticed under Dyson as an architect, he was loyal to the design. Mukai did much of the work himself with one skilled worker, Eddie Garcia, and paced the project over 27 months. Mukai's perfectionist tendencies may have cost us time, and more money than pre-fab, of course, but within our modified budget. In the end, the

Above: Insulated hallway at Taliesin West.
Photo courtesy of the author.

Creek House, in the 1980s, took 18 months and went over bid by 20 percent (my patronage of the art of authentic architecture).

I contend that cost constraint can foster creativity, and it's so satisfying to solve a problem within our means. On both houses, Dyson employed cost-trimming moves. On the Creek House, he called out common materials and standard sizes wherever possible; for example, standard slider glass and barn wood siding with one-by-one bats to cover and define the seams. The front is designed with common shakes, but the pattern, although labor and material intensive, makes it extraordinary. Karl Ashley Smith, architect and architectural writer, describes in the January 1990 *Fine Homebuilding* some specifics of the framing that might interest builders and structural engineers:

> At first Dyson thought the house would best be framed around laminated wood arches, but a couple of phone calls revealed that just the cost of laminated arches, without sales tax, delivery or erection, would double the framing costs. Since economy was a high priority, Dyson turned to plan B: frame the roof like a gable—only with a curve at the top instead of a peak.

[The contractor, Greg] Potter and his crew [Dave Friesen—both had apprenticed with Dyson] began framing the gable ends atop 6 x 12 beams that double as the second-floor top plates. Curving pony walls were nailed on top of these beams, with the studs on 24-in. centers. To calculate the curvature, the crew drew a full-size replica of the gable on the shop's concrete slab floor. That allowed them to measure directly and get accurate stud lengths, as well as the appropriate angles for the top cuts. The curving top plates are made of five layers of 1 x 6, glued with construction adhesive and nailed at 6-in. centers.

At the ends of the house, the curvature of the roof slopes down to meet the lower curve rising up from the first floor. At the point where these two meet, the roof is cantilevered nearly 9 ft. beyond the end wall of the house. With laminated arches, supporting this overhang would have been no problem. But with no arches, supporting the pointed ends of the roof posed a challenge.

Dyson's solution was, in effect, to extend the structural gussets—the crew called them "beaks"—beyond the end walls to support the overhangs. These gussets consist of 5/8-in. plywood sheets that link the curving 1 x 6 plates. Along with 2 x 6 studs between the gussets, the assembly works something like a box beam.

The assemblies transfer the loads of the overhangs to 6 x 6 posts in the walls.

After the gables and gussets were completed, 2 x 10 rafters were installed, spanning between the gables and installed tangentially to the curve of the top plate on 24-in. centers. The rafter placement was critical because, to center the plywood sheeting correctly, the rafters had to be spaced on 24-in. centers at their outer edge, instead of at the inner edge where they attach to the plate.

The installation of the rafters on the lower curve was done in a similar fashion, with one notable exception: on the upper curve, the rafters were toenailed into the plates, but on the lower curve Simpson "H" series hurricane anchors were used.

Above: RiverHouse windows are segmented to suggest a curve.
Photo courtesy of the author.

Dyson creatively employs standard materials for non-standard purposes. My favorite example is the decorative beam ends on the Barret-Tuxford Residence, which are actually lowly toilet floats. With an unlimited budget, we would have curved north and south walls so the footprint resembled a leaf. In compromise, we curved the wall of the great room to frame the river and the Sierra foothills beyond, but rather than pricey curved glass, segmented storefront glazing and standard sliders perform an illusion of glass that's curved. The front maintains the illusion of curve with an arced fountain and curved concrete entry. (See illus. on p. 102–4).

Other owners have similar stories. Tom and Sue Jaksha recognized how expensive it would be to import enough dirt to build up the substantial berm on one side of their cliff-hanging house, so Tom, whose work took

Above: *Poles with colorful streamers greet a bride waiting on the terrace to walk down to the ceremony. Photo courtesy of the author.*

him around the countryside in his truck, collected tires and broken concrete as landfill. The site has a minimum square-foot requirement (theirs is smallest in the association), so the overhangs compensate—Sue recalls, "That's how the house got its shape, but budget-wise, we couldn't complete the entire plan, so we designed it in phases with the roof over the future master bedroom and French doors with a two-by-four across them because it dropped off five feet from there with no decking." When Kurt Zumwalt balked at the cost of massive outriggers on their house in Madera, Kurt, a builder himself, wanted to lop them off. Instead, Dyson suggested he construct them hollow and paint them white to match the rest of the impressive home. Same thing with the fireplace: when an 8-foot fireplace cost five times a 4-foot fireplace, Dyson designed an 8-foot horizontal element to incorporate the 4-foot unit. Zumwalt also described their "fenestration compromise." Art wanted windows floor to ceiling, but the couple insisted on a whole house fan and opening perimeter windows for airflow. They settled on low opening windows below the solid glass that don't impede the view. In Ken Woods' first Dyson house, Dyson designed the foundation *around* a beautiful, sculptural rock. With wildfire a fear in the California foothills, the metal roofs on many of Dyson's buildings are not just cost-effective. On the Baughman Residence in Springville, the metal roofing was laid diagonally so leaves and other debris from the oak trees wouldn't accumulate. The metal roof was also a solution to a pesky woodpecker problem. Sometimes a problem can be turned into an asset. When Stan Gould, one of Art's early bosses, wasn't quite sure how to mask a row of poles in a shopping center he was designing, he told me Art suggested they top them with flags.

Many of the architects I spoke to relished the challenge of "unbuildable lots" (like the Creek House). In the Sunnyside neighborhood of Fresno, Dyson client Brett Runyon found a triangular sliver of land an older couple had used for a garden—not large enough for an ordinary house. When the husband died, the wife couldn't take care of the garden, so Runyon asked if he could buy it. "The obvious view was on the back [industrial side] of the Sunnyside Country Club," Dyson explained. By angling the view towards the greens, they blocked the blight and maximized the narrow view. The day he told me this story, I noticed his whiteboard featured a quote by Moliere: "The greater the obstacle, the greater the glory in overcoming it."

There's a spirit of pride in a common creation. I've been on lots of building sites where the builders joke around and have fun, but they are often talking about anything but the routine task they're doing. The attitude is, "That's good enough." (When my husband worked construction as a teenager, they used to say, "Can't see it from my house"!) Conversations I've overheard on Dyson's jobsites often involve puzzle-solving feats, stories about previous problems marvelously mastered, challenges about how level or what a perfect fit, bragging about a job well done. Even before it was finished, the Lapp RiverHouse was joyful. The builders laughed constantly, and their good spirit permeates the walls.

With an extraordinary home, the subs take extra care and boast about their work. When we reluctantly told the cabinetmakers we couldn't afford to curve the kitchen island, they volunteered to curve it anyhow and use the photos for their advertising portfolio. Similarly, the drywall is smooth (more expensive) for the price of texture because the guys agreed it would show off their skill. It doesn't cost more to groove the detail lines they call "reveals" at *exactly* 8 feet, 4 inches, but the entire home is so noticeably balanced that one guest, an expert in Eastern philosophy, said as she entered, "This is completely Zen."

Sometimes it's an illusion. It would be lovely (but too expensive) to have an infinity edge on the pool, but by setting the far edge of the pool lower than the close edge, it looks like an infinity-edge pool connecting to the flowing river. With the glass above the interior 8-foot walls, the house looks much larger than 2,000 square feet, and the mirrored backsplash visually expands the kitchen.

When Eddie Garcia was pouring the concrete at the RiverHouse, I asked if we could sink PVC pipe in the cement bench to create a series of tubes along the edge. Easy, he said, and now we can insert poles with colorful streamers when the event requires fanfare.

Art Dyson invited Greg and me to accompany him and Audrey to the 2016 awards ceremony of the American Institute of Architects, San Joaquin chapter. We were all braced not to win, since Art had kind of cleaned up at the previous awards ceremony two years prior, adding to his wall of important awards, including the Residential Housing and Shelter award for the Creek House in 1989 when John Lautner and Joseph Esherick were judging. In 2016, AIA judges Andrew Dunbar, Jason Silva, and Jana Itzen awarded the Lapp RiverHouse an Award of Merit, and the Award of Excellence went to Dyson's Hilton Residence. What made me exceptionally proud was the comment from the judges, articulated by Donald Munro of *The Fresno Bee*, that the RiverHouse was built on a strict budget—because it certainly was. We made careful and judicious choices, stayed inside our budget, and the house still won awards from AIA and SARA.

As an aside to architects, I'd like to make a point about the impact of bold design on an architect's reputation. Dyson told me, "I knew early on that the kind of work you started in was probably going to be the work you did for the rest of your life, so you don't want to settle." Harvey Ferrero told the cautionary tale of a talented architect friend who found himself doing "cheesy little strip malls" for developers. "So finally one of the developers he worked for wanted to build this huge, palatial house. So he came to my friend and said, 'Joe, do you know a good architect who wants to do my house for me?' And he wouldn't even consider Joe, because he felt Joe only did flat work" and was incapable of doing something unique. "What I always thought was that I would never do anything I wouldn't want my name on." He said, "The price didn't bother me, unless it was totally unrealistic. If they wanted a house and they wanted a piece of *architecture*, then I was really willing to do it, and I rose to it." Ferrero said he was especially drawn to the challenge of small houses. "I think it's incumbent upon us architects to be able to do decent modest architecture." Most of his work came from people who had seen something he designed. "If you can get a reputation for doing something good, then [your clients have] friends who may be of like minds. Just like the story with Joe, you know, they looked at his work and thought he couldn't do a house they'd want to live in." ▪

CHAPTER FIVE:
SOUL SEARCH: PLANNING A SPACE WHERE YOU'LL FEEL UTTERLY AT HOME

Above: Morning light in the kitchen of the Lapp RiverHouse.
Photo by Scot Zimmerman.

"To accomplish great things, we must not only act, but also dream; not only plan, but also believe."

—Anatole France
(on the white board in Dyson's conference room)

I f a house is to reflect the owners and the setting, the architect must invest in understanding the clients and how they interact with the site. Dyson says he relishes that "detective" role. "I study people," he says. "When architects build structures for zoos, they study the animals, but many architects never study the people they're building houses for. Most architects," he adds, "don't know if their client is right- or left-handed." Over the course of this project, I have had the privilege to meet some extraordinary architects, many of whom have connections to Dyson, Frank Lloyd Wright, or Bruce Goff. Not surprisingly, their take on planning similarly involves client analysis from the head right down to the soul.

Not only do the architects have to get to know the clients, but the clients have to know themselves as well. The time spent looking, talking, sharing ideas, "playing house" in various spaces pays off. Planning a house is like planning a wedding: You could elope, which is the romantic equivalent of a studio apartment—you're married; you're housed. You might choose a 90-minute Las Vegas wedding package, predictable as a tract home. The über-elaborate, right-out-of-*Bride Magazine* wedding correlates to the McMansions that crowd the foothills around Fresno. Sometimes one person plans the entire nuptial event and the other just shows up, or (and this is where I'm going, obviously) you could plan together intimately, both of you, selecting just the elements that will be meaningful to you and your special guests, that reflect and amplify your lives, values, and commitment. My admonition is exactly this: if you're a client, find an architect whose work you admire, maybe someone whose work isn't all the same, and utterly open yourself to the planning process and the self-revelation that entails. Be honest. Don't hold back—it's your own private space you're planning. Allow yourself to trust, and align your imagination with the professional who is unfolding your singular space and creating your design. Dyson writes:

> At the core of American life there is an irony especially visible in architecture. On the one hand, we have the right to explore and express our own vital and individual freedoms. Yet the means of production for a building are in general socially collaborative, influenced by the value judgments of others who may never use or even see the product. Sameness, possibly flawed or mediocre, is frequently preferred and enforced by cultural practice. Difference can be deemed untrustworthy. Having the pluck to navigate these often overt but sometimes hidden tensions requires a determined and resourceful client. The architect who has such a client is indeed fortunate.

So, architects and students of architecture, I implore you to design bravely as you simultaneously learn to intuit your clients' lives and personalities. Learn to teach your clients, guide them into a vision that will amplify their dreams. You can design for people's lives as they live them if you ask questions and try to see the world as your clients do.

PLANNING THE CREEK HOUSE

"We depend on our surroundings obliquely to embody the moods and ideas we respect and then to remind us of them."
—Alain de Botton, The Architecture of Happiness

When Scot Zimmerman introduced Dennis and me to Art Dyson in that brick office on P Street, I brought my graph paper drawings and explained to him what I'd drawn and why, and I complained that my tilted A-frame of an elevation just didn't work.

I picture this conversation happening in the Creek House at the dining table, but that's impossible because it's a planning meeting for that house.

Art corroborated that it was in his office; we were sitting on one side of a table, and he sat across from us. "We need to lengthen out the lines," he said, smoothing his hand in an arc, as if over an expectant mother's belly. "And then come back in," he continued, scooping both hands together to meet, cupped at his heart. The house looks like that—as if it has erupted gently out of the river bottom, as if next season it will burst into flower.

Over two sessions, he asked a battery of questions that had less to do with form and more with preferences in music, art and food, the patterns and rhythms of our lives. He asked about our dissimilar backgrounds: I'd grown up in an upper-class suburb of Los Angeles, my father is a successful L.A. lawyer, my mother keeps a lovely home and is active in the community; my family all have advanced degrees. Dennis's family struggled to farm cotton and grapes; his father died while we were dating. While Dennis's brothers, Ron and Gary, graduated in engineering from Fresno State, Dennis, after studying ecology at community college, took a program in horseshoeing and became a farrier because he was drawn to the challenge and independence of the traditional craft.

Although it was the 1980s, you might have called the two of us "hippies." We wanted to live an organic life in tune with nature and off the grid.

Dyson asked what houses I remembered admiring as a child growing up in San Marino, a town that looks like you're driving down the streets of *Architectural Digest*. I'd loved the O'Connor's Spanish style house, but I said I didn't want something Spanish—not here in the forest. Dyson says the curved entry originated from the idea of a Spanish arch.

On his hand rendering of the elevation, because we were newlyweds, Dyson drew a mock picket fence encircling the house and a very cool sports car for Dennis with the same "female" lines they both admired in automotive design. He joked that he'd build a whole tract of them, flip-flopping the façade down the block.

Above: Rendering of Lencioni Residence by Arthur Dyson.
Photo courtesy of Mark Hammons.

PLANNING THE RIVERHOUSE

"The house shelters day-dreaming, the house protects the dreamer, the house allows one to dream in peace…"

—Gaston Bachelard

As soon as we'd purchased the property, I started drawing floor plans, this time incorporating the Steinway and a long cupboard to store 50 black padded folding chairs. Limiting the design to exactly 2,000 square feet, I tinkered on the drawing well into the night, leaving my masterpiece proudly displayed on the counter. When I woke up later than usual, I was dismayed to see Greg drawing and erasing on *my* plan. He had made a little graph-paper-and-cardboard piano, dining table, bed, and easy chair to scale, and was altering *my* design! I had to admit his changes were good ones, though, and that I'd have to get used to living with another creative in the house.

For many reasons, Greg and I went directly to Dyson when we were ready to build. Greg had been living in the Creek House (Lencioni Residence), but he hadn't yet met the man who designed it. We emphasized our restricted budget, yet our desire to work with him within our means. Again, I had brought the graph-paper floor plan Greg and I had drawn together. We had no clue about the elevation. "Are you still getting along?" Art asked and told the story of a couple who had brought in a draft floor plan carefully taped back together. It seems they tugged and struggled until the plans ripped in two.

Art's more efficient now, but no less thorough: Art emailed a 30-page questionnaire reminiscent of the interviews 30 years prior. The questions are comprehensive, and I share many of them in service of designers, architects, and clients becoming more in tune with their surroundings. The subtitles are mine, but if you adopt any of the questions in your practice, you should cite Arthur Dyson, not me.

The exercise, in and of itself, feels like art therapy. All the ideas come from you, but you didn't necessarily know you thought that until prompted. For a couple, it's like marriage counseling. Art says the *way* clients fill out the form is revealing. Some print, some write in script, red ink, black, or pencil. Art said some are funny or clever; he's had people tell him that they cried when they read some of the questions. One client, he said, realized that when he grew up his only safe haven was at the dinner table, "'otherwise people were yelling at each other, people were squabbling.'" It's emotional. "Folks are giving you the inner blueprint they walk around with," he says. "So it's really easy for me; once I have that, just to put it all together."

Greg and I filled them out independently before comparing answers and were not too amazed that our responses were eerily similar (we met on eHarmony.com, after all). The introduction of Art's questionnaire begins:

> The design of a new home is the most personal experience in architecture. While we spend most of our lives within the embrace of architecture, decisions about what and how we experience a building are usually made by other people long before our arrival. Frequently, pressured for time in this hectic modern world, most of us come only rarely upon a moment of conscious perspective about our reactions toward the architecture by which we are constantly surrounded.

What do these unique clients consider beautiful, what thrills them to their core?

The first question has to do with beauty. Dyson writes, "Surrounding ourselves with beauty has been a fundamental of good living since ancient times." He quotes Plato: "For he who would proceed aright...should begin in youth to visit beautiful forms...out of that he should create fair thoughts; and soon he will of himself perceive that the beauty in every form is one and the same." He could have quoted his teacher Frank Lloyd Wright, who said, "If you foolishly ignore beauty, you'll soon find yourself without it. Your life will be impoverished. But if you wisely invest in beauty, it will remain with you all the days of your life." In her book *Tales of Taliesin*, Cornelia Briarly writes, "Mr. Wright—like Emerson—felt that 'Beauty is its own excuse for being.'" I had the great fortune to speak with Briarly—by then, 98 and the matriarch of Taliesin, and she told me, "Mr. Wright considered beauty the highest form of morality."

So, clients, really consider what beauty is for you. And, architects, listen. Built landscapes are rarely neutral; they either add or detract. Beauty in this world is receding as Big Boxes, housing tracts, and storage units proliferate and displace open space. Because individuals have different ideas and images of beauty, *uniformity*, by definition, cannot be universally beautiful. Dyson argues that any competent draftsman can design a good building, "but it is someone that can touch the soul of an individual that creates beautiful architecture." The introductory paragraph of a piece Dyson wrote, titled "A Search for the Soul of Architecture," begins like this:

> When one thinks of architecture, one generally thinks of buildings and of walls, as architecture is generally defined as the art and science of designing and constructing buildings…for me, architecture was never about buildings, but about the individuals who would occupy them.

Ferrero laughed out loud when I read the title of that piece to him, but his friend Dyson takes the soul search seriously. When Jim Wasserman interviewed Dyson for a *Fresno Bee* column in October 1995, the writer described this elusive search for "soul" in art. "The conversation became quickly indistinct, roundabout, and vague—in the way of art and about the way things are. And about how we live as human beings," Wasserman begins. "Known for the offbeat, [Dyson] was talking about being adventurous. And romantic. About writing and poetry, mystery and paradox, beauty and soul, and all those things that seem visibly downplayed in city life today." When Wasserman asks, what a house *should* look like, Dyson says, "[A]rchitecture is not the repetition of something learned but, rather, the exploration of something sensed, for extending the boundaries of human experience and understanding," for understanding what *each* client feels his or her own house should look like.

When Dyson asked for our definition of beauty, I responded literally: "Taking the startling elements of nature and condensing them, arranged just a little off-balance," while Greg was more philosophical, writing, "Beauty is a real and open expression of the truth of God." We were to list things we find beautiful:

Deb: The most tingly, beautiful experiences of my life involve an unusual cast of light and shadow: Looking out over moving water morning or evening, there's a stillness in the air which contrasts with the current; or the way a wild fig tree wraps around an oak and the transparent backlit leaves contrast with the burley trunk. Where rough meets smooth and shiny there is often beauty. I love the yellow undulating hills of the Valley with dark green oaks and granite outcroppings.

Greg: Whether in personal contacts or when watching a stage play, sincere feelings are beautiful. When Harold Hill stops Winthrop, who is angry there's no band, Harold Hill says, "Hey kid. I always think there's a band." I cry every time.

What is your client's relationship to space?

Walk into a building with clients and observe how they orient themselves. I gravitate to a window or a zone with high ceilings, but some people crave cozy corners. Dyson suggests that architecture is experienced as "a time sequence when individuals travel around and through the space." He points out the obvious, that human beings are kinetic by nature, and as such alter the perception of scale and the rhythm of a space. A building is much more than its photograph, yet, as in a photograph, negative space is at least as important as positive space. Each has a dramatic impact on the inhabitants. When I imagine our house, I don't imagine it empty and static; I always see it full of people—who's in it? Greg and me; Greg, me, and the kids; holiday crowds; friends at a concert or a dinner party? Even during the 2020 shelter-in-place and ensuing semi-quarantine, friends and family escaped the confines of the city and sat 10 feet from us on the terrace overlooking the river and the foothills to connect, console, and catch up. In anticipation of any event, I glide imaginatively through the house anticipating the dynamics of flow. As Frank Baughman, whose home graces the cover of *The Architecture of Arthur Dyson*, says of his house: "The house is exciting to look at, but the *experience* of space is what's special. It is very *livable*." I was fortunate to observe the flow from inside to outside and from room to room, downstairs to upstairs, and out onto balconies overlooking the foothills when the Baughmans lived there, and also with Susan Peck and Dana Gillespie, the second owners—thrilling details at every welcoming turn. Similarly, at Dyson's Jaksha Residence in Madera, with two successive owners, I noticed that the space from inside to outside and between all the rooms is so fluid and punctuated by the unexpected. I have experienced this in both my houses, different as they are one to the other. Always I am half-cognizant of a dance as I move into, out of, and through the built space. Greg and I attended a benefit for the public radio station at the home of Kurt and Terri Zumwalt, designed by Dyson. We attend this event every year, always in some lovely, well-appointed home, but conversation sometimes flags, and people tend to get a plate of food and perch on a chair to wait for the program. At the Zumwalts', people moved from room to room and out on the terrace. Groups of two and three melded fluidly, and a single person felt free to join a conversation, most of which were about art and architecture. Zumwalt, a general contractor, is pleased with the outcome: "I can understand from plans how a building is going to look from the blueprint and the sections, but I can't understand how it's going to *feel* with the light and the space. Art is particularly good at anticipating the feel."

To engage space to nurture aspirations, Dyson asks about our dreams and what we'd like to achieve spiritually. I wrote that I wanted to relax and accept that I am not in control of every aspect of my life (building a house, by the way, is excellent practice for this quest). Greg hoped to create a community of family and friends where all are welcome, encouraged and fulfilled, including himself.

We realized from Art's probing ("Consider how a room, area, or space might facilitate those desires...What adjustments could be made to find a truer orientation with what you believe is most important?") that we need separate, discreet workplaces to create, and a completely separate spot for bills and taxes. In fact, Greg composes in his Tree House studio above the existing red barn, and I settle in the living room ("like a studio," I wrote, "but not warren-like—open, with lots of glass"). If Greg is cooking, I migrate to the window chair in the bedroom. We concluded a separate desk in the hall for business would prevent us from being annoyed or distracted from our creative pursuits.

Art asks, "What will your life look like when your dream is achieved?" Greg's will continue the path he's on, he says, but "with more confidence and vigor," and if I can balance the dominant social side of my personality with a private need to create, I'll be amazed, but pleased.

The questionnaire asks us to consider where we spend time, which activities take place where, and how each area relates to another. He encourages us to consider the passage of time and seasonal needs. We chose similar words to describe what we wanted our home to be (open, connected to the outdoors, flowing from space to space, warm, calm, light, elemental). He asked about the impression of the house as you drive up to it, and we both answered "in harmony with the landscape," and "elegant, yet playful."

Art asks questions anyone might ask, such as: "Which rooms have you most enjoyed in previous homes or vacation houses?" but he asks questions which evoke deeper contemplation: "Think back to your favorite childhood spaces." The house I grew up in was a stately white colonial in a neighborhood of lovely lawns and shade trees, big back yards with swimming pools. Sensibly, my younger sisters occupied the bedrooms upstairs near my parents, and I, the eldest, stayed downstairs. But the boxy little space made me a little crazy. My bedroom, originally a maid's quarters, had a louvered window onto the driveway facing the neighbors' brick wall, and a high, vine-covered window that faced the garage roof. I would fantasize about replacing the wall that blocked off the garden and the pool with glass. Once, when my parents were away, I talked my youngest sister into trading rooms with me. Annie's room had large second-story windows looking out through a liquid amber into an elegant oak and over the neighboring houses north and east. (We had to switch back when our parents returned. Perhaps I've been craving windows ever since). Greg's parents ran a church camp, so the boys slept in open-air cabins all summer, which Greg loved; accordingly, our bedroom's wall of 18-foot tall windows allows for stargazing from bed.

It seems there's a balance between retaining cherished elements and opposing less-favored elements. Dyson gives an example of an aversion from Charles and Lela Hilton's home in Florida. Art suggested a metal cool roof to deflect the heat and keep a clean profile, but the Hiltons wouldn't hear of it. In their childhoods, metal roofs covered the shacks of the poor and didn't belong on their mansion. Similarly, he says barn wood siding can evoke nostalgia for some, but not for farm families, who generally crave an interior that's sleek and clean. Dennis had grown up in a tiny space, where rooms were multipurposed by necessity (his bed was in the laundry porch; he did homework standing at the washing machine), so Dennis insisted on a separate and private office.

Page 7 launches into "Space Exercises" for each room in the house: first qualities, then activities, and there's a similar battery of questions about the site: Why did you choose the site, what are the positives and negatives, what features do you want to emphasize or avoid, how important is privacy? He asks about sun angles, the yard and outdoor activities and asks for favorite photos of vistas on the lot. Every architect I talked to assumes that site is an essential consideration. Larry Brink said,

"Your site you've chosen has particular views or certain amenities that need to be taken advantage of instead of bulldozing everything down so it's flat and you can put down some sort of box on it."

"With Mr. Wright, you learned how important nature is, how unique the site was, and you fit the personality of your building to your site as well as to the person you're building it for." At Eric Lloyd Wright's site perched above the Pacific Ocean, the fluid cement structure nestles into the cliff like an eagle's aerie. Wright said both architect and client have to become intimate with the terrain and the views, and assess the possibilities.

Dyson says an architect must respond to a site as Native Americans have. He says you need to listen to "the songs of the site: the songs the birds sing will tell you the secrets of the site, which way the wind blows and which way the water flows on the site." He says, "The answers are all out there. You just need to take the time it takes to look for them." When I asked Mickey Muenig, a Goffian architect in Big Sur, he said he defers to the site. He told me he camped on the site of the Post Ranch Inn for a calendar year as he was designing the Post Ranch guesthouses. He suggested that the delays in design and plan check we perceived as frustrating were actually advantageous because we had the opportunity to observe our site over all the seasons.

Every site offers challenges of the elements and vulnerability to natural disasters. Earthquakes and flooding were considerations at the Creek House, so it's built up 3½ feet to compensate for the high water table, and the curved roof hunkers it down for stability. Because the RiverHouse is in a wildfire zone, we avoided wood and chose a cool metal roof. Wind coming up the river canyon required copious steel clamps to keep the roof from lifting off. In hurricane-prone Florida, the sand dunes informed his design of the Hilton Residence, but the house built on sand is formed of concrete. It was designed to withstand 160-mph winds with the wood deck on steel girders, and it has withstood several hurricanes to date.

Determine your clients' relationship to natural light and sound.

Architecture can shield your clients from nature (from harsh elements, for instance), but good architecture can maximize the residents' exposure to its positive influences, shift of light and sound, and the animation of the wind. Our needs in the hot, dry Central Valley of California differ from my daughter and son-in-law's in the Catskill area of New York, yet we can retain our relationship to nature despite our climatic requirements. With a solarium that celebrates the elements in every season, they reinforce their connection to the forest, which reminds my daughter of the forest outside the windows of the Creek House where she grew up. We both appreciate architecture that integrates the built and natural landscape making seamless where one ends and the other begins. Gaston Bachelard quotes George Spiridaki, who rather poetically expresses the way architecture can seem to him:

> *"My house is diaphanous, but it is not of glass. It is more of the nature of vapor. Its walls contract and expand as I desire. At times, I draw them close about me like protective armor....But at others, I let the walls of my house blossom out in their own space, which is infinitely extensible."*

Authentic architecture celebrates angles of light at different times of day and of the year. Kevin Burke and Carrie Meinberg of Parabola Design call their Charlottesville, Virginia, home *Timepiece*, which is built around that celebration. In a text, Burke writes:

> *As its name suggests,* Timepiece *functions as a sundial. A beam of sunlight focuses through an oculus and traces its way across the walls and floor of the home's northern-facing Observatory. Timepiece is oriented true solar north/south and many of the building's angles—including walls along both staircases and the parabolic curve of the north-facing roof—are determined by the movement of the sun throughout the year, from its shallowest point at the winter solstice to its steepest angle in the sky during the summer solstice.*

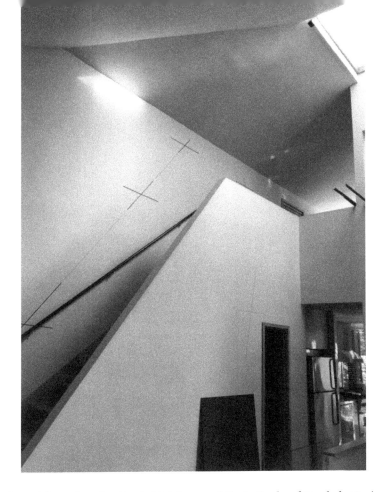

Above: Timepiece *by Carrie Meinberg and Kevin Burke of Parabola Design.*
Photo courtesy of the author.

Kevin credits Carrie with this concept of allowing light to determine
the plan, "evolving built forms from natural forces rather than human
aesthetic conventions." In a whimsical application of this notion, at a
home in Oakland with a commanding view overlooking the San Francisco
Bay, Dyson designed a concrete monolith *immediately inside the entry*—not
to block the incredible view, but to focus it. As you open the door, a small
aperture in the wall directs your eye specifically to Coit Tower, where
the couple first met. In fact, Dyson proposed a monolithic partial wall

Above: *Morning light on the Lapp RiverHouse dining table.*
Photo courtesy of the author.

at the RiverHouse to delay the dramatic view of the river, but we are not that cagey—and wanted to move furniture at will. Windows and skylights reach for a view or edit out a scene Dyson and his client would rather avoid—this explains the sharp angles on some of his houses. "Too many homes are isolated from their natural surroundings—the soaring rooflines [in Dyson's designs] are in response to view lines or view corridors," he explains, "not random aesthetic tricks. Without stars and sunsets, without access to the out-of doors," he contends, "you don't know whether the wind is blowing or if the birds are singing, or if it's raining or if there's a sunset. We try to bring those things back into the buildings." I have described so many prism-light moments or moments when the light dances across a room, but each seems extraordinary and new.

Will Green, second owner, with Cliff Schiesl, of Dyson's Barrett-Tuxford House wrote in an email that he felt "both grounded (the house is half underground) and connected to sky. The windows on the south side are 12 feet tall and the moonlight bathes the entire house. It's a great compliment," he says, "that the deer haven't figured out that this is a place where humans live." Before living in their Dyson home, Green's complaint about the architecture that surrounded him ("as a human *spirit*") was that architecture, in general, felt "so detached from the earth, and so temporary." Green says that, because the house is sited in the trees, when people come up their driveway "they feel like they've entered into not just a different world but a different reality." He adds, "The most common reaction when people enter the home is an audible gasp. People look like they've just entered a cathedral and become quiet."

Dyson says, too, that architecture has become significantly more impacted by auditory interference. "With the introduction of energy standards that prevent not only thermal transfer, but the natural sounds of nature," he says, "we are further disconnected from our biological origins." The questions about sound are standard at first: What natural sounds do you enjoy? Which sounds displease you? What house noises do you normally pay attention to? But there are three particularly interesting ones: "If you could have any sound for your doorbell, what would it be? If there were any sound in the world that you could delete permanently, what would it be? What single sound might you want to give everyone as a gift?" Greg wrote, "a contented sigh," which, like Green and Schiesl, is what we hear when people enter our house. I said I'd give the sound of a running river, so a fountain bubbles by the RiverHouse front door because the water sounds connects the house aurally to the flowing river beyond. Also, the timbre of water matches the timbre of traffic, and we'd prefer to ignore commuters who drive past morning and evening.

Normally, the sounds coming from the park across the river are pleasant, but the fountain can also mask disturbing music if the campers decide to share.

In "A Search for the Soul of Architecture," Dyson writes that arboreal sounds "harken to our primordial memories of a safe environment absent of predators." He writes, "the wind in the trees, the rain, and other echoes of nature provided calming patterns which resonated with the human heart." He told Wasserman, "Look how people exercise today. They work on their hearts as a muscle in health clubs instead of taking a walk in the woods to exercise their hearts and their souls. Most people live and work in environments that are containers for human beings, [intended] to screen out the elements. People rely on a world of images with no depth and no substance." Dyson laments that the "songs of nature" which once soothed us are today replaced by "the harsh mechanical noises of garbage disposals and air conditioners." I wanted to build a house without that mechanical noise. Many call that noise "white," but I find it distracting and disturbing. White noise, like a white lie, is probably benign, but it still undermines absolute authenticity.

Let the discussion about lifestyle be candid

Perhaps the most interesting section is the Lifestyle Inventory. He separates the two parts of that compound noun when he says it: life-style, as in the *style* of your life, the *way* you live. Clients who haven't known Art well have said this was startlingly personal at first; yet, they all realized in retrospect that the answers guided important design choices. Dyson writes:

> How you live, both daily and in longer cycles of time, determines how spaces in your home need to be arranged and configured. In a general sense, lifestyle is just the way you go about being at home. Personal traditions, family habits, and cultural inheritance are some of the many aspects of lifestyle. The constellation of activities you enjoy or honor, from private individual occupation to public social gathering, deserves to be served as fully as possible by the structure you build.

He asks about how we spend our time, favorite pastimes, typical weekday, morning, evening, weekend, personal activities, group activities, outdoors

Above: Upstairs interior view of the Creek House.
Photo courtesy of the author.

Above: The great room in the Lapp RiverHouse is endlessly convertible, depending on the occasion. Photo courtesy of the author.

activities, provisions for pets, exercising, entertaining, overnight guests, working at home. Little did we know just how well the RiverHouse fosters working from home until we both taught all our classes online during the COVID-19 pandemic of 2020.

Spaces must be created out of the way they'll be used, and all the artist-architects I talked to consider the client's lifestyle. Larry Brink, who apprenticed with Dyson under Frank Lloyd Wright, said understanding and interpreting the client is something both he and Dyson absorbed from their mentor. "I also am interested in how the people live. 'Do you entertain, do you cook, do you like music, do you garden, what are your interests?'"

In an interview, Eric Lloyd Wright agreed that the architect needs to know how an owner occupies space. When I asked how he conveys those ideas into design, Wright said, "If they like music, it's got to work acoustically, and if they like to entertain there has to be provision for that, but the living room still has to function for living." Listening to the client is crucial, said Wright. He praised Dyson for his listening and his intuition. "He's very good that way—it's one of the things that attracts me to him. He does have this concern [for the client], which is what a good architect should have, but most of us don't because usually we get so wrapped up in all the problems of building and understanding what we're trying to do."

What things are important to your clients?

People have a lot of stuff—too much, certainly—and too much of it is left *out* for lack of storage. Planning can go a long way towards having a place for everything based on frequency of use. Good design facilitates judicious editing of things, so that only the most meaningful are on display. Dyson asks: "What furniture, artworks, and/or artifacts do you wish to feature or put in special locations?" One young couple, who had good artistic sense, but little experience collecting art, weren't sure why Dyson designed a niche in their front hall. Dyson told them to place a nice rock there to envision the space and observe how, at certain times of day, the sun would feature that spot. By the time I saw it, the moon illuminated a wonderful sculpture by a local artist that "suddenly spoke" to them. In Cusco, Peru, we learned the Incas designed their windows in such a way that the sun spotlit particular niches on significant days. If the Incas could do it, so can you. "We can use light to illuminate or warm a space," says Dyson, "but we can also use it to reach the hearts of the occupants." He tells the story of some clients who did collect fine art, but when he asked what they would take first if they had to evacuate, both pointed, without hesitation, to a pair of goblets their children had given them for their 25th anniversary. "So, obviously, we put them in a nice place where they could be seen, but we also made sure that, by means of a clerestory window, the sun would shine in through that window and hit those goblets at 3:00 PM, June 5, the date and time of their wedding." Greg and I have slim attachment to things, but we did need specific room for the grand piano away from the light, and natural light for reading was a high priority for us.

There's a whole page on music, computers, media, and art. Television, unimportant to us, is relegated to the den. For us, live acoustics are critical. The open plan and acoustical curve is ideal for concerts and salons for up to 50 people. Dyson client and sound engineer Carl Casey said in an email:

> Audio engineers have known for a long time the unfortunate effect of parallel walls—a phenomenon known as standing waves. These waves emphasize certain audio frequencies. That's why the walls in sound studios are nonparallel. The same is true in most of Art's houses. In fact, I use the Dyson-designed bedroom to record singing.

Dyson asks about built-in furniture, so we were able to anticipate the bank of cupboards with countertop in the living room for the fifty folding chairs, and the built-in benches with drawers that flank the view windows both inside and out.

Ten pages are devoted to Room Planning with an introduction that encourages multipurposing. "A creative and engaging architectural solution need not be confined to familiar limitations," writes Dyson. Multi-use is a guiding principle in the RiverHouse: piano and concert hall, yoga studio, writer's workspace, library, wheeled armchairs, kitchen, dining room, den, and guest room all coexist in 1,000 square feet, fully half the house. It seems silly to me to designate a single purpose to a room so that it waits in pause mode until awakened like the personified candlestick in *Beauty and the Beast*. My childhood house had an entry hall, formal living room, family room, den, formal dining room, and a breakfast table in the kitchen. My family lived in the wood-floored family room stepped down from the white-carpeted living room. The entire wall facing the tree-ringed backyard, patio, and pool was glass, and a green and leafy buffer separated our house from the neighbor. That room had a game table (where I often did my homework), fireplace, and bar. It occurred to me around middle school that those rooms could easily be combined, and I sketched plans, which rearranged the downstairs with fewer walls (and a fully-fenestrated bedroom for me!).

Dyson opens the section "Living Spaces" with an observation: "Modern life tends to be more casual and informal than in earlier decades. Just as the formal 'parlor' of late Victorian times passed away in favor of a 'living room' in the twentieth century, contemporary uses of interior domestic spaces are also evolving." He asks about the function of the living room. "Is it a place for adults only, adults and children, or a special occasion area?" For seating arrangements: "conducive to formal discussions or more intimate conversation?" Is the focus inward or outward? What activities? What about storage?

Either he tired of the questionnaire, or the bedroom questions made him bashful because Greg skips eight pages here, deferring to mine. As Art writes, "Bedrooms tend to be the most personal, private, and intimate spaces in a house. Most people spend at least one third of every day sleeping, and these spaces also commonly become personal refuges for rest and relaxation." The questions range from sleeping schedules and habits to size of bed and the "feel": "Do you prefer a cozy, confined sleeping area for your bed? Do you generally prefer a light or dark bedroom?" Is it a "suite," with a sitting area, fireplace, deck or garden, or a desk? "Should the master bath/dressing area be designed to allow one person to shower, dress, and leave without waking the other?" How much closet space?

He asks which areas should have most direct access from the bedroom and most separation. Art supplies several options for multipurposing the additional bedrooms, and our guest bedroom doubles (triples? quadruples?) as library, media room, and den.

For the bathrooms, Dyson asks for principal users, location, and desired features with suggestions: a view of the outdoors or not, small and enclosed or open and spacious, shared or private, single room or compartmentalized, bright and sunny or cozy and softly lit, many decorative objects on view or uncluttered? Based on observing their wives taking out the blow dryer and other morning-routine items on busy mornings, then watching us pack it all up again (or leave it out), Greg and Art came up with a lift-up counter with electrical plugs inside, so I can lift up the top of the counter, dry my hair, and close the top back over all the tools of beauty.

Art invites the client, 23 pages in, to determine "a personal pattern of activity." Yours or your clients' will reflect your personality or theirs, but you can see the pattern:

> *Where do you spend the majority of your day?*
>
> (by the windows in the living room)
>
> *What does your everyday work environment look like?*
>
> (same)
>
> *Where do you sit in a restaurant?*
>
> (on a patio or a table by the window)
>
> *What is your favorite way to relax or unwind?*
>
> (a glass or a book on the terrace)

Ask for clients' preferences in other arts.

Many of the architects I have known consider clues and cues from other art forms, so it's critical for a client to be unabashedly honest in discussions about art. Your preferences can inform an architect only if your responses are authentic; responding with what you think you *ought* to like will be distracting or misleading.

Dyson has told me much of his inspiration derives from writers and people in the other arts. "We have such a huge palette to work with as architects. We have form and line and texture and color and rhythm...materials... space. A writer can take a bunch of letters and arrange them on a piece of paper in a way that can make you cry, make you laugh, can make you melancholy." I suggest a writer doesn't have to worry if an imaginary house will stand; no physicist tested Daedalus and Icarus's wings made of wax. Undeterred, Dyson continues: "If somebody can do this with letters and paper, think of what an architect can do with a gigantic palette." He devotes several questions to reading—"Do you? Where? Which authors, books, magazines?" He himself had loved Joyce's *Portrait of the Artist as a Young Man*, the way cadences of the language change. He asks, "Were you read to as a child? By whom?" and he asks for a favorite childhood story. (Greg said the musical *Seussical*; my favorite was Kenneth Grahame's *Wind in the Willows*.)

He asks about favorite movies, plays, or performances and where we see them. Our choices are overwhelmingly hopeful and a little romantic: *Les Miserables, Billy Elliot, Romancing the Stone, Guys and Dolls*. I'd say that optimism and romance are clearly reflected in the architecture of our home.

Eric Lloyd Wright likes to know what poets the client favors. Sitting in his workshop, where he's made sure we have a sweeping view of the Pacific Ocean over the Malibu cliffs, Wright quotes from Rumi's "The Wine and the Cup": *Moonlight floods the whole sky from horizon to horizon*, and he adds, "How much [light] can fill your room depends on its windows and the way you look through them." But that's Wright; Rumi doesn't do as much for me as, say, Wallace Stevens or Mary Oliver. Good architecture is as structural as poetry. Karl Ashley Smith, an architect in Southern California described for me his concept for "eloquent tiny homes" he calls "Haiku Cottages." Your choices can inform structure, motif, and style.

Dyson asks explicitly for a client's musical tastes. He told us that Debussy was Bruce Goff's favorite because the work is athletic and light, whereas Mr. Wright liked Beethoven's heavier and more monumental works. In the conversation about music, my musician husband said he might choose Bach if he had only one book of music on a deserted island because of the music's complex elegance; but if he had to teach one work every year for eternity, it would be Debussy's "Trois Chansons." He says: "It is passionate. It is simple, yet not easy to learn." Myself, I like Santana and David Bowie, which I'd say is also passionate, simple, yet not easy to learn. Comparing architecture to music, Dyson said we generally appreciate discord leading to resolution in music, but people are reticent to introduce dynamic elements in architecture. Without a bridge or occasional discord, how square and repetitive music would be—that formulaic jingle that nags you all day and all night. Brink said in an interview, "Organic architecture is far different than just 'architecture.' It's Mozart [compared] to computerized *whatever*." Greg says that the closest metaphor to composing music is designing architecture. "You build the frame first and add the details later," he says, and compares composing a longer-form musical piece, with its themes, motifs, and structure with *composing* a home. Musician and writer Howard Rappaport explains that conductors speak about the *blueprint* of the score, "the plethora of details they must synthesize and begin to imagine in their heads before actual rehearsal begins." The blueprint, to a conductor, includes both the musical symbols on the page and "the mental, aural, and musical impression that is forged upon the conductor's brain." Goethe famously said, "Music is liquid architecture; architecture is frozen music." While the comparison to music is apt since the participant has to move through architecture to activate it, just as music must be played in order to thaw, in *Organic Architecture: The Other Modernism*, David Pearson writes:

> *Organic architecture is living, rather than frozen, music, performed in the continuous present. With its juxtaposition of harmonies and discords, its diverse rhythms and syncopated movement, and its asymmetrical proportions and structure, it has closer affinities with modern music than with classical compositions.*

The structures of music and buildings are comparable—the theme that begins in one place develops in another with motifs and variations. Contemporary philosopher Alain de Botton writes, "Buildings are choirs rather than soloists; they possess a multiple nature from which arise opportunities for beautiful consonance as well as dissension and discord."

Be prepared to read between the lines.

I've come to understand that architects can learn to sense how a client will grow into a space, not out of it. The architect has to be a bit of a therapist, perhaps, encouraging a timid client beyond what he or she can conceive. It starts with an inquiry into the clients' "yearnings," as Harvey Ferrero called it. Ferrero said Goff always insisted they start with the clients' preferences and encourage them to reveal individual priorities and styles. "You give them a house that they want—only they really don't *know* they want it yet because they don't yet have the imagination to envision that, so you do question them about certain things." Sometimes Wright, or Goff, or especially Purcell, Dyson said, would talk about a project that wasn't as *powerful* as other projects, but the architect knows in his heart where he's taken it. "When you have a client who has expectations that are pretty ordinary because that's what they can conceive, and you reach up here," holding his hand chest-high, "that's great. You [the architect] might be able to conceive up here," extending his arm fully, "but the measure of success is the distance between what the client originally could conceive and the result." He described times when people had pedestrian expectations, and he tried to take them too far, hence a brief portfolio of unbuilt work.

Ferrero says he encourages clients to bring in clippings and photos of places they like. Asking questions about those clippings, he extracts their yearnings. Post-Usonian Project's Matt Taylor describes a conversation with Frank Lloyd Wright's client Mrs. Pew. At first she'd "hated" her house and felt Wright had utterly ignored her preferences.

After two years, Taylor recounts, Mrs. Pew was ready to sell the house at a loss, but decided to "give the house a year without struggling with it." On *Post-Usonian*, Taylor explains:

> In that year, a transformation took place. She discovered that "Mr. Wright had not built a house for who I was—but for the person that I could become. It turned out that Mr. Wright had listened well and understood me very deeply."

Dyson says someone who comes to him with a colonial home in mind doesn't actually want all that's implied with the dated design (no indoor kitchen or bathroom, no air-conditioning, plantation masters and slaves, for example). Dyson says, "Maybe they're looking at the monumentality of it or the monochromatic color scheme...you try to find out what they like about it, and introduce something that's more representative of today's materials and today's climate and today's energy problems, their values, and their contemporary way of life." Dyson's Andrade Residence is a good example of this.

Brink says Mr. Wright taught them to design *appropriately* for the client, "understanding what [the client] should have, maybe not what he thinks he wants per se, because he's still thinking inside the box." A California client who brings in photos of a Spanish castle may yearn for thick walls and walkways, arches, curves, and fountains, says Dyson. "An architect can take those elements, materials, and shapes and rearrange them in an authentic, modern vernacular, perhaps around a private garden at the home's center, in harmony with the California heat." When Art saw the agricultural site for the Gerringer Residence, he assumed they'd want to look out at the picturesque vineyard. But the grape farmers had plenty of that view all day from the seat of a tractor, so Dyson designed a circular house facing inward on a courtyard and pool at the center, an escape from the dust, hot sun, and noise from the fields outside.

Above: Dyson's Andrade Residence.
Photo by Scot Zimmerman.

Above: Art Dyson.
Photo by Scot Zimmerman.

At one of his "Archilectures," Dyson looked out at some of his clients. "One thing I've been fortunate about," Dyson concluded, "I've had clients willing to look at alternatives. They are 'wealthy'—maybe not monetarily, but with a wealth of spirit and adventure. I try to show the impetus and inspiration behind these homes." While Dyson praised his clients' "wealth of spirit," it's thrilling to see him freed from tight budgets. In Seacrest Beach, Florida, perched on the Gulf of Mexico, Dyson designed a grand home for Charles and Lela Hilton. In an interview, the Hiltons said they were drawn to the water, so water and waves are a dominant motif. Deborah Wheeler, in a July 2001 *Walton Sun* article quotes Lela: "'Charles is a water watcher. In this house, even though you're inside, you feel like you are outside.'" To bring the feeling of water in, Art designed wave-like curving walls, and round windows like a ship's. Walls of windows open out to Gulf views from every room. Wheeler describes the home's free form, "looming," she writes, "both horizontally and vertically. Sweeping lines dip and curve, stretching across the two distinct wings of the house." Art told me he observed Lela's jewelry, "complex, expressive, free-flowing," and he references those forms in the design as well. The house mimics the waves and the sand dunes and Lela's favorite pelicans in flight. "The gray concrete walls round and weave in and out, much like the Gulf waves the home overlooks." Did the reporter intend a set-up line when she asked how many square feet were in the massive house? Art answered, "There aren't any square feet."

"We've never made an attempt to be different, but our clients are different," Dyson says, attributing all his work to a third-person collection of collaborators. "My objective is to produce a design that will enable my clients to fulfill their potential, and to live and work in a most meaningful way. Hopefully with order, clarity and harmony we will arrive at a solution that is both practical and beautiful. My clients," Dyson says, "are very courageous because they dare to go against the tide of fashion. They've allowed us to create a setting to care for their souls."

Above: Mike Kelly's remodel of the Leverich Residence.
Photo courtesy of Arthur Dyson.

When I ask Dyson's other clients to recall their planning experiences, they all relate similar versions of the same theme. In an interview, Diane Leverich remembers, "I gave [Dyson] three criteria: make the house open, massive, and airy. While my design in my head was so amorphous, Art was completely in sync with the vision." Diane said, "I would love to have the whole world understand they can have so much more *design* in their life. It matters. It's food for the soul. The soul needs to be fed." Her husband Veldon added, "In a way, it's like religion. Some religious views are quite advanced over conventional or simplistic views, but the people that identify with [complex, advanced views] have to be at a certain place in their life for it to be meaningful. Otherwise it's anathema to them. I think it's the same thing with architecture," he said. "You have to get to a place where you're ready for something like Art Dyson's designs."

When Bill Kelly bought the Leverich Residence years later, several architects looked at the renovation job. Kelly said most told him, "'Here's what I do.

Here's my building that I can design for you in this spot.'" Kelly said Dyson asked what he liked—his favorite color, childhood memories. He said he went to lunch with Audrey and Art at a restaurant with a similar view, and Dyson made sure that Kelly sat facing the view and asked him what it was about the view that moved him. Kelly was impressed that Dyson had enough confidence not to invest his own ego too heavily in the project, but rather let the design reflect Kelly's personality and lifestyle. Pamela, Bill Kelly's wife of seven months when I spoke with them, said, "This house is completely Bill." I had heard "completely *built*," which made sense to me, for instance, as a poem is "complete" or "achieves form," but when I asked for clarification, she altered her comment—"It's Art Dyson, of course, but it's *so Bill*."

Sue Jaksha remembers questions about lifestyle, art, and music, but was mystified by questions such as: What is the first room you enter when you come home? and How much time do you spend in the bedroom? "At first I didn't realize what this had to do with designing a house," she said, laughing. Because the Jakshas work away during the day and often travel on the weekends, the house was primarily an evening house for the two of them—or 40–50 people. This meant one large room with the kitchen, dining room, and living room reaching out at different angles. Where my houses are both curvilinear, theirs features dramatic reaching angles designed to maximize the view within the restrictions of the housing development. Sue said Dyson pulled out a piece of paper and drew a circle, "This is where the sun would set." He arranged the line of sight so the dining room wouldn't block the view of the sunset from the kitchen, and he drew another circle, and another, and from this schematic evolved the floorplan. Karen Bosch, a librarian involved in the Fresno County Library design, described and shared with me the same circle-and-line-of-sight discussion.

Fred Stitt, of San Francisco Institute of Architecture, praised Dyson for spending extensive time with the clients, "acquainting himself with the essentials of their lives, and especially of their aspirations. Other architects," Stitt said, "even well-renowned ones, will first show what they've done and awards they've won before ever asking a question of the client, and [intimately investigating the clients] is the *first* thing Arthur will do." Ferrero said the same thing: he named some "superstar" architects who, he said, want to give you *their* house, a house they designed in their style, not specifically for you. In an interview, client Ron Evans said he was introduced to Art Dyson by a potential architect for the job who, once he heard that the Evanses wanted to do something *different,* said they should talk to Art instead. Evans said Dyson told him and Ruth Ann first about his philosophy and asked them about what they liked: what art, what music, how they lived, "and he *listened* to the answers," Evans told me. "We thought, this guy is great; he's going to build something just for us." The Baughmans said something similar regarding their first interviews of architects: "We were quite distressed because we thought, 'How can we get a house the way we want it when they won't listen, and we don't know how to build ourselves?' Then we met Art."

Dyson asks us to speculate about the future. "Will our children boomerang? Will they bring grandchildren? Will our parents move in? What will our retirement look like?" Our prescience was tested and confirmed one year when my son's ex-wife needed help getting on her feet, so she and her children (whom we loved as grandchildren) moved into the Tree House studio for a semester. The kids had the run of the outdoor garden and pool and patio, but we could still work inside in peace until I called them in for dinner. Dyson asks about hobbies in the past, present, and five, 10, 20 years out. He asks how we would like to see our lifestyle changing in 10 and 20 years. I thought long and hard about this because Dennis and I didn't even have children when we built the first house, and twice I became too cramped in the Creek House and chose to move from that lovely space. Barring a catastrophe, we don't think the children will boomerang or our parents will live with us, and the den or the Tree House can handle visitors. Family and friends come visit more often for *their* vacations, but that's what we hoped would happen.

In answer to his question, we both said we thought we'd spend more time at home creating (and we do, especially since we've now retired).

Dyson asks for a single color to represent yourself. "For most people, color has an enormous importance in the experience of architecture," says Dyson. "Personal surroundings reflect emotional patterns and tendencies through the presence of hue, tone, and shade across the spectrum of visible light." He spends a page discerning a client's response to color and another for sound: "Sound is a natural corollary to color." That may well be, but Greg turned to me when we were filling these out and said, "I care a lot about a lot of things, but I have very few opinions about color." Certainly, there are some things people care about, and some things they don't. Fortunately, I have enough opinions about color for both of us. I asked which he associates with him and which with me. He chose deep blue for himself and bright yellow for me. Hmm. I also chose dark blue for him, but for myself I chose blue-green—blue/gray. I think I always aspire to be calmer than I really am, so I chose cool colors to respond to that yearning.

Art's next question comes with the guided imagery: "Close your eyes, feel wonderful, all your senses are satisfied. What color comes to mind?" When I followed his instructions honestly, I was filled with a golden yellow. Greg wrote "swirling purple and brown?" then said out loud, "I really do have some sort of block related to color." For the next question, "What colors leave you indifferent or have no particular impact," we both eschewed pastels. Greg makes a good point: "Tan/brown in my lawn is depressing; the golden tan on the hillsides is beautiful; brown in an ale is glorious. Everything has its place." Art asks what color exudes strength: "Feel strong;" he writes, "everything around you is supportive of well-being. What color gives you that feel?" I wonder if different clients answer this differently because we both wrote deep blue. The last color question is about security: "Envision yourself completely at peace, restful and safe; you want for nothing; you have it all. What color comes to mind?" Why do I say gray? What I can say is the dominant gray we've chosen for the walls inspires deep confidence and security.

Art's interest in psychology is most evident in the final section on Heritage and Relationships.

> *Who we will become is often greatly determined by our reaction to where we have been. Our experiences in the past have a strong bearing on what we look to find in the future. This set of questions looks back over the broader scope of time to examine the oft-forgotten, and sometimes hidden, things that have brought alive the present urge to build a home.*

He asks about favorite and least favorite childhood activities, including smells, tastes, or sounds. "When you were young, what kind of places did you dream about having as a home—e.g., castle, cave, forest?" (I imagined our church, St. Edmunds, repurposed as my stone and stained glass home.)

Before the RiverHouse planning commenced, Art and Audrey Dyson came up to the site for a picnic. That August evening the water was high and lazy. We talked about how to orient the house to maximize the views (*I lift mine eyes up to the hills*) and how we could take advantage of shade from sycamores. We were already sensing the hypnotic effect of the river—hypnotic, but constantly moving in one direction, as does life. We wanted the house to become a part of the setting without interrupting it. Unlike the Creek House, the RiverHouse would be visible from the road, so we hoped to integrate the profile of the house into the landscape following the foothills' silhouette.

Art brainstormed the form of the house with cardboard models. I scribbled "Spring '08" on photos Greg took of rough cardboard models arranged on Art's conference room table. One looks like a croissant, the layers of roof lapping one on top of another like pastry; one squats like an Anime sumo wrestler. I know Art doesn't like similes, but the forms were all evocative of one thing or another. I was having trouble picturing this house as our prerequisite "simple and elegant"—especially simple.

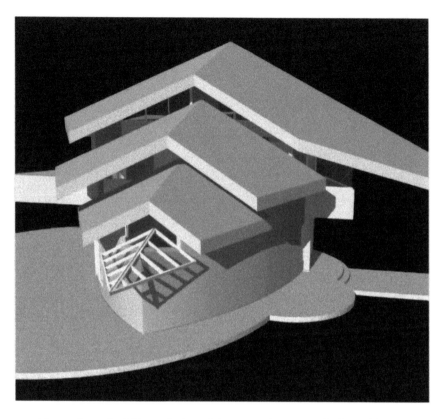

Above: An early CAD rendering of the Lapp RiverHouse ("The Trilobite").
Courtesy of Arthur Dyson and Associates.

The resulting design was stunning: a massive, elegant, trilobite with a cascade of clerestory windows down its back. It had swollen to 2,800 square feet, but the additions were thrilling, even if we weren't sure we needed a master suite that grand. I especially loved the loft office with a pop-out glass-cornered window looking up to the foothills and the way the clerestories would certainly shift the angles of light at different times of the day and year. Secretly, we knew it wouldn't make budget, so we calculated how far we could stretch, up to 25 percent over the original figure. I filled a couple pages of a legal pad figuring pricing scenarios, we determined our ceiling, and put it out to bid. ■

CHAPTER SIX: BETWEEN DESIGN AND BUILD: ASSEMBLING THE TEAM (AND SURVIVING PLAN CHECK)

Above: View of Creek House balcony.
Photo by Scot Zimmerman.

"Nouns are the ashes of verbs."

—William Gray Purcell (1880–1965)

A rt Dyson contends that the transition from design to build, in fact, the whole planning process should include the builder. While his logic is infallible, builders are reluctant to get involved. They don't have time to spend planning—they're builders; they want to build. They have a better working concept of the cost of materials and labor involved in a design than the rest of the team, but the architect and the client make the give-and-take decisions about what's worth skimping or stretching on. Ask a builder if the most outrageous idea can be built, and the answer is almost always, "Well, it *can* be…" with a poignant trailing off of the voice and "here we go again" implied in the ellipse.

Frank Lloyd Wright sent apprentices out to live on the sites as they oversaw the construction of his designs. In *At Nature's Edge: Frank Lloyd Wright's Artist Studio,* Henry Whiting describes Wes Peterson's role in overseeing the original building in the '50s. In the '80s, Whiting sought out the same craftsmen as he refurbished and repurposed the studio as a residence for himself and his wife Lynn Fawcett Whiting. In imitation of Frank Lloyd Wright's model, we ultimately chose, for both houses, contractors who had apprenticed with Dyson; in this way they had a preexisting relationship with the architect, and, having drafted for him and worked in his offices, integrally understood his philosophy, style, and core ideas.

So many of the owners tell stories of frustration with contractors who either don't get the artistic choices or don't value the artistic choice over the "feasible." Will Green explained, "Many contractors just couldn't figure it out, couldn't see the vision we had, couldn't deal with the lack of right angles in the house or the rigid instructions I was handing out. I came to understand the challenges Art [Dyson] and Bruce [Barrett, original client] encountered...economic, aesthetic, physical, emotional. I came to understand that the whole *process* is organic, not just the design."

Without involving the builder in planning, the bids may not align with your budget and the plan. In the '90s, I was subpoenaed to testify on Art's behalf. It seems a couple had hired Dyson to design a certain home with a certain budget. When the bids came in higher than the budget, they refused to pay Dyson for his work. In the meantime, they built a paint-by-numbers mansion. Art's counsel called me up and asked if I would testify, which I was glad to do. He announced at the hearing that my house had been built on budget, which, of course, it hadn't been. When I told the true story (and nothing but the truth), the judge leaned towards me and asked, "Was it worth the overrun?" I must have looked at him incredulously because when I said, "Oh, yes!" everyone kind of chuckled, the couple blushed, and Dyson won the case.

We had our own frustrating case in our second Ranch House remodel. The plan we envisioned was straightforward, we thought: turn the attached garage and shop into a living room and office, move the front door from the side to the front, and build an attached garage off to the side. So we went to Dyson with a simple sketch. Dyson's conception, channeled through a group of young apprentices, resulted in bids *four times* the budget we'd brought to him. I would have gone back to the drawing board, but Dyson was busy with Taliesin, and Dennis refused. So Dennis and a handyman, Bill Barnes, made the changes I had drawn on graph paper—all with the original roofline and only slightly modified footprint—and we paid in cash as we went.

You can do that too, of course, if you trust your own design, and if you have someone you trust to execute it. Oh, I *know* the compromises we made, and I see the amateur features. Had the west-facing windows been southwest and clerestory, I wouldn't have had to buy ordinary blinds to cover the flat sliding glass doors when the sunset assaults the west wall. We would have been drawn to sit and talk in the living room Art designed more than we ever did in my vast converted garage. The spaces I've inhabited before and since, designed by Dyson, are more stimulating, more interesting, more integrated into the setting. I compensated for the compulsory right angles with a circular entertainment center, a built-in bench, and ordinary sliders connecting us to the outdoors.

Our contractor for the RiverHouse in 2009 had also been a draftsman in Dyson's office. After an intimate 28 months with the man, it's impossible to separate the building of the RiverHouse from Sidney Mukai, but we had originally narrowed our choice of contractors to six. The first two showed us mansions on "The Bluff" over the San Joaquin River in Fresno, which were massive and well-crafted, but showed no recognition of Dyson's sense of design—so they were out of the running. After experiencing such a disconnect between our vision and the expression of the first two contractors, we decided to meet potential contractors at the Creek House as a fair but revealing litmus test; and they would know what they were in for. If we spoke the same architectural language, we concluded, then we could go see their work. One contractor drove up to the Creek House and started shaking his head in awe as he stepped down from his truck. He held his chin, as if to control the shaking, but he shook it all the way up the stairs, through the whole tour, and as we came down the stairs towards the massive glass and wood front door, he said, "I couldn't do this," and laughed in defeat.

Steve Soenke had been working on a Dyson remodel in Fresno and became somewhat involved in the planning of ours. His craftsmanship and design details on the Fox-Wosika Residence impressed us. We appreciated his articulate expression, his talk of world events, and his border collie Hank, who played well with our Queensland. A contractor on a project like this lives closely with you over a year or more; it's critical to feel comfortable in each other's company—even better if your dogs get along. Mukai was busy with a big project in the mountains out of town. We started to think of Soenke as our guy.

Tingling a little in excitement, we pulled up to Soenke's office in Fresno's Tower District, also a Dyson design—an aborted restaurant project the contractor cleverly converted with a lot of style—bold color, drop spot lighting, seven matching panels of abstract oil paintings rescued from another Fresno restaurant failure. Hank greeted us with exuberant wagging, and Soenke ushered us inside the airy, open office for the bid. We sat down, smug that we'd decided not to be shocked if it was up to 50 percent over budget.

The design was brilliant; the contractor was skilled—we could swing it. Soenke set down an elaborately tabbed and indexed bid. I noticed he took a step back rather than sitting as well. He launched an item-by-item explanation, but I impatiently flipped to the last page. The bid came in well over twice what we'd planned. The steel bid alone was almost the budget for the house. Suppressing any reaction and ignoring a roaring inside my head, I picked up the bid folder and walked back to the car. Through the glass wall, I saw Greg stand up, look at Soenke, then at me; then he strode out and joined me. "No one will be at Art's this late," I grumbled. Greg asked what I thought, but I couldn't answer. I recalled the project I was forced to drop in the '90s as we drove in silence. I had to have appeared rude to Steve and cruel to Greg, but I had to think. We had choral rehearsal that evening, and I had one class in the morning before I could talk to Dyson. Distracted and still calculating, I sang half-heartedly through the Durufle Requiem, and I spoke, still in monosyllables, to Greg on the way home. He remembers me waking him up in the night and saying, "So, if it's twice our budget, we'll slice off the top half."

Having slept little, I wore a Reedley College sweatshirt and jeans to my Friday morning class and went straight from class to Art's. "How did it go?" Art asked optimistically, rising to meet me when I burst in the door. I went straight to the conference room and slumped in a chair. I said the same thing to Art that I'd said to Greg in the night, my hand slicing the air: "We have to lop off the upstairs." I told him the total bid and price per square foot. It's hard to unsettle Art, but he was as shocked as we were. I know I began talking too fast, detailing what I'd considered all night: "We'll make it one story; it has to get back under 2,000 square feet; if it's single-story, do we need all that steel? The downstairs is the important part—if we just bring the master bedroom downstairs..." I didn't want to destroy his design, but we simply couldn't afford it. He said we'd start a one-story design immediately.

One thing Dyson says he learned from Bruce Goff was an enthusiastic attitude about revision; when Goff had drawings returned, he responded "with a sort of glee: 'I get another chance to really get it right!'" But Dyson said it wasn't easy for him to learn. He had once designed a fireplace for a woman, and she just didn't like it. At first Art was provoked—that design was perfect! Some time passed before she asked for another design, and he realized he was excited to have another shot at it—and the second design, he said, was immeasurably better.

RiverHouse, Take 2: One story and 2,000 square feet *exactly*. We were even happier with the elegant simplicity of the one-story elevation. We wanted four bids, but we could only gather three builders we liked. No one in 2008 would consider a contract like the one we'd had in the '80s. It would be "cost-plus," but all three promised they would work with us to keep costs down. Steve Soenke, of the first draft, was one; we were still impressed with his professionalism, wit, intelligence, and organization, even though Art thought his bid might still be high. In our neighborhood out in the Sanger river bottom, Kevin, a local builder was remodeling a locally designed organic 1940s home with built-in furniture that looked out onto Collins Creek. The craftsmanship was beautiful, true to the pseudo-Wrightian design, and our neighbors and the subcontractors were all content. Because he lived out east of town as we did, we thought Kevin might have a competitive bid, and we had to consider price. Kevin said his brother designed organic homes in Colorado, so he was not frightened by the style. The third was Sidney Mukai, who had been the general contractor on Dyson's Geringer House, a Creek House contemporary. He was an architect-builder himself and had been an associate of Dyson's in the 1980s, so, to the extent it's possible, he understood the inner workings of Art's mind; perhaps most importantly, Art was partial to him personally. The day before the bid-opening ceremony, I'd told Greg that I also favored Sid. I like the Frank Lloyd Wright model of apprentice-on-the-job. The Geringer House Sid built is a sensible masterpiece. It boded well for us that he knew design as well as building, and he does most of the work himself. He's Buddhist, I added; a little Zen might go a long way.

The day before the momentous bid-opening ceremony, we picked up Soenke's sealed bid from his office. We chatted with him blithely and said we'd call tomorrow. Kevin was going to drop his off at the house on his way home from the job in the neighborhood, and Sid, who lived near Art's office, was going to drop it off there. We came home late from rehearsal, and there was no envelope from Kevin. A message on the answering machine: "I'm sorry," the message began. "I was so excited to work on a house like this that I didn't consider all the other obligations I have committed myself to. I have too many projects going, and I have promised work for family. I know I'll regret this, but I have to withdraw my bid." We were disappointed because we had wanted four bids for balance, had reconciled ourselves to three, and now, with only two, we wouldn't be able to adequately gauge high and low bids.

Friday morning in Art's conference room, the lone envelope from Soenke lay in the center of the conference table. Greg paced. Art told jokes. I tried to laugh along, but the two-bid prospect seemed teetery, *and* at 9:00 (the deadline) Sid's bid wasn't here. We stalled and told stories. "Remember when you bid out the first house—the variety of bids?" Art reminisced.

At 9:30, we couldn't stand it any more. We'd left messages for Sid, but he hadn't answered. "Let's see what we have here," Art finally said (we were relieved that he'd been the first to cave). I opened the envelope slowly, then dropped my elbows onto the table and spread the message between my hands so they could see: "I respectfully withdraw my bid." Greg exhaled in a nervous laugh. Art simply pronounced, "Well!" Before I could wilt in despondent anguish, my cellphone rang. Sid was on his way. We all but froze for the minutes it took him to travel the few blocks between his house and Art's old office.

Sid stood nervously in the conference room doorway. Even though the ceremony had deteriorated, I thought at the time it was important to keep up the appearance. I looked at Greg and Art and told Sid we'd call him later that day.

Sid's bid was reasonable, and our relief was extraordinary. He was clearly the only man for the job.

So we had a contractor; next step was the building permit. When I'd done this 25 years ago, it had been a quick process. Greg Potter had sent me in with the plans and told me to smile. At 50-something, that ploy seemed not only inappropriate, but probably ineffective.

Planning offices are suspicious of difference. Ron Lucchesi, an architect for Fresno County says he has to look closely at designs from Dyson: "They're just not ordinary," he said. Before Ann Zimmerman knew her husband Scot (the photographer who introduced us to our architect), she was working at the County. She told a story at dinner with the Dysons: one of the inspectors in planning came to her desk and said, "Ann, you like weird and interesting things. You have to see this house." He meant the Creek House, of course, where we were eating paella as she spoke. "Hunh," Art said under his breath. Ann quoted her colleague in a deep voice: "Look at this house—doesn't it look like Hobbits belong here?" "Hunh," said Art. He loved it, she told us, but he added, "This will be a *job*." "Hunh," Art repeated for the third time.

When I turned on the tape recorder at the planning desk and asked Lucchesi about Art's work, his comment was that the buildings need space. "They're different, so it's better when they're not surrounded by ordinary houses."

Being a space junkie myself, I tend to agree. I prefer any house to have ample breathing room. Too many homes feel crowded next to each other like a restless mob. But Marc Dyson defended his father's in- town designs: "I think it's cool to have an angle jutting out in the midst of uninspired architecture. You're going down the street and suddenly you're pleasantly surprised." The Evans Residence is one that comes to mind. Paula Landis remembers growing up in the neighborhood: "Most of the houses were and still are unimaginative. So when the 'Cootie Catcher House' with its peaks and dips in the roof line went in, it was a dramatic change." Dyson told me the contractors kept putting a cross on its highest peak.

Sid was finishing a project out of town, so he couldn't start until November. I was impatient; as teachers, we were anxious to get going while it was summer break. But Art consoled me—it'll take that long to get all the paperwork done, he said. Indeed, I filed for a permit in July. It came back for extra engineering in September. By that time, our engineer had quit engineering to teach high school math, so we found a substitute. We resubmitted. The County demanded more specifics for which brackets and what type of air conditioning system. We repeated that there was *no* air-conditioning. Lucchesi agreed there was no need, but we needed a water test to check flow so close to the River. At first, the guys at Rasmussen Pump learned from Irena, the engineer at the County, that the test could only be done at low-water mark in September. By now it was November.

Rasmussen, bless them, managed to convince Irena that the water was low enough for an accurate test, so we wouldn't have to delay almost another year; still, they were busy, so it would have to be after the holidays.

Tuesday, January 12, 2010, I mustered my courage. Greg had and I arranged to meet Ron Lucchesi at the County for *another* shot at passing the permit. We had picked up the revised engineering plans from the new engineer, who had done a careful job with clear details overmarked in red. At Art's office, we reattached engineering plans to the official three sets. Before Sid even got there, Ron Lucchesi started ticking off the changes which Paul, the new engineer, had indicated very clearly in the margin with page number references and special annotated details. Several satisfying *RL* initials filled the circles around certain items: *check!* Then we came to the corner connections where Paul had still called out upside-down brackets. Again, Lucchesi paused. Heat crawled up my neck. "Can we bring the engineer here?" I asked. "He explains it clearly: he has shown that the load is carried this way, so it's stronger upside down. He says it doesn't really matter— there's minimal load on that joint in any case, but his professional opinion is that it should be upside down." Greg enjoined, "It's just a bracket. Why don't we put one right side up and one upside down?" Lucchesi shrugged and smiled. "I'll have to talk to my supervisor."

One time, Dyson was pulling the permit on a large house for a family with seven children, so he had drawn a bedroom wing for the parents and a long wing for the children's bedrooms with a second children's staircase. When the second staircase wasn't allowed, Dyson took the plans and made some changes, then returned to the County.

Where the label had read "staircase," he had instead written "sculpture." When the permitter asked what the sculpture was made of, Dyson replied, "metal staircase components." "But it's a sculpture?" the permitter asked. "Oh, yes," said Dyson, and—stamp—the plans were approved.

Sid joined us, and the three of us paced the government office as if we were awaiting a delivery in a maternity ward. In a way we were: we needed this birth, so this baby could get on with the business of growing. Sid said, "We *know* there will be modifications in the field. We just need to get out there." I asked for change for another dollar and walked down around the corner to feed the parking meter. I returned and Greg walked outside for air. I tried to play the game I play in my head of visualizing different activities in the house, but it was hard to concentrate. Lucchesi returned and discussed the mischievous brackets with Sid. They pulled out the massive Simpson Catalogue of brackets and braces. "This just gets bigger and bigger every year," commented Lucchesi. Everything gets bigger—plans didn't used to be 29 pages long. Sid and Ron found a heavy-duty bracket they could agree on. Sid labeled the specific bracket and signed on each of the three official plans.

We waited: What next? With utter understatement, Ron flipped through the sheets of corrections to make sure he hadn't missed any, then muttered, "That's it." Sid looked at me silently, but his eyes conveyed exclamation. I, likewise, side-glanced at Greg. Then Ron smiled at Greg and me and said, "Now it's time for the *music of the stamping*." What a delightful phrase! "How are you two at flipping pages?" he asked. "Expert," said Greg.

"Let the wild stamping begin!" While Sid took out the actual permit under his contractor's license, Greg lifted a page, I lay it flat and Ron stamped each page, "Approved" (!), 87 stamps in all. We rolled two sets of plans up, one for Sid and one for us, and Ron carefully folded the County's set in a complicated origami around the booklets of certification for engineering and energy and soil. I headed for the glass door; Greg was already outside.

But Sid, ever patient, reminded me: "First you have to pay the County." ■

CHAPTER SEVEN:
FROM THE GROUND UP:
SOME STORIES OF
THE BRAVERY OF BUILDERS

Above: *Framing the Lencioni Residence.*
Photo courtesy of the author.

"[Men who make houses] look at a problem and think, How can this be done? And come up with one or two preposterous ideas. And then they actually do it, and if that's not sexy, I don't know what is."

—From "Men Who Make Houses"
by Linda McCullogh Moore, *Sun Magazine*

Framing a house is usually dramatic. Crops of houses sprout on the outskirts of Valley farm towns that surround us. I'll drive by a pad with footings in the morning, and by evening the proud skeleton of a house stands in all its gangly glory. Framing the Creek House, however, presented some challenges. I recall three capable men lined up side by side, window frames to their right, looking down at the plans and up at the sky and back again, scratching their heads, visualizing and articulating options. Greg Potter, the builder:

> *How are we going to attach these "beaks" which are cantilevered out to the square portion of the house, and get them to stay fixed to the house? It wasn't detailed on the plan. We made those beaks out of plywood, nailed them off—it became a type of beam that attached to studs in the corners. With the laminated top plates that acted as a strap from the point of one beak all the way across the roof all the way to the other side and held everything together.*

The downward swoop of the top curve, where it meets the upward swoop of the lower curve creates a space behind the chimney that with less imagination would have been an unreachable attic. From the outside, it's obvious that the space completes the line that unifies the whole design. In the eventual realization inside, the line is retained, only interrupted by a two-sided chimney wall. What goes up there, you ask? Maybe daydreams and incubating ideas.

An unusual design requires persistence and ingenuity to build. This chapter includes examples of joy and frustration. Years after building the

Above: Curved shop wall and "beaks" of the Lencioni Creek House
Photo courtesy of the author.

Creek House, Potter recalls: "I was new to construction, so I knew no fear. Oftentimes I had people say, 'How can you look at that design and build that?' I'd say, 'How can I not?'" Having worked in Dyson's office, he understood Dyson's design: "If Art calls for this type of finish, it has to be this finish. If not, you're going to blow the whole design." Potter said some of the structural details were left for them to figure out in the field. "'Your house [the Creek House] is built custom piece by piece because of all the different sizes and shapes. The rounded roof meant every stud had to be separately measured and angled to match." He laughed. "Some of the details were tricky: How do we come up with a rounded top plate? The curved cabinets offered a 'fun' challenge. The skylights in the garage area were a challenge. We laid it with string line out so the planes would be right, and we made cardboard templates to make sure it would fit."

Above: Steel banisters by Dennis Lencioni.
Photo courtesy of the author.

Potter said, "It's not necessarily lacking in the design, but a builder just needs to do his homework. I had to go back in to Art and say, 'I have some cantilevers here that aren't being supported. What I think we should do is...I need your blessing.'" It helped that Potter and his right-hand man, Dave Friesen, had both been draftsmen with Dyson, and Friesen was studying for his contractor's license. Their youth and optimism were clear assets. "We were all young," Potter said. "It was edifying strategizing with Dennis because he was always positive—we'd find a way." Their spirit pervaded the whole project. I was writing a short story at the time which featured two characters strikingly similar to Potter and Friesen. They read it standing shoulder to shoulder, looked at each other, and Friesen said, "I think it needs more description." Potter improvised: "With his muscles rippling," flexing his biceps, "his wind-tossed hair falling on his tanned shirtless shoulders." They were fearless physically, hoisting each other up in our backhoe bucket to reach high and awkward areas. Potter said he didn't think he could build the house today without encountering prohibitive OSHA restrictions.

Dyson likes to get the client involved in the construction of the house, if possible. I pounded in my share of nails on the roof of our house where my "roses" wouldn't show. Dennis, however, was a blacksmith, who had built gates and a stock trailer from scratch. When Art asked him if he could weld, Dennis answered yes, meaning he knew how to join together two pieces of metal. What Art had in mind, Dennis dubbed the "Berthas" for their heft and extraordinary weight.

We lived next door, so I was on the jobsite daily (advisable, to the extent possible), grading student papers or cleaning up in an attempt to be useful and speed things along.

Since Sheetrock is another dramatic step, I was paying close attention the day the drywaller was about to close off the curved end of the bedroom, bringing it back to the dreaded dead square. I asked if the wall was load-bearing. When he said it wasn't, I asked them to stop and Sheetrock the curve, resulting in a graceful curved ceiling, one of the most dramatic elements of the master bedroom, accentuating the arc—and gaining 25 percent more floorspace and a more inviting approach to the balcony.

Working on a contract was financially frustrating for Potter. He was especially frustrated by subs. "They'd give you a bid, then you'd carry that bid in your budget, and then when it came time to do the work, they'd pull out." The unusual design scared some away. "You can fight them, you can sue them and waste more time and money. Or you can just do it yourself." He could afford to keep Dave Friesen working with him for about half the job until Friesen got his contractor's license and started working on jobs of his own. Ultimately, an older friend of Potter's, Carson Daley, who had taken three nephews under his wing, came out to help him finish. "If it wasn't for Carson, I don't know how I would have finished the house. I was disillusioned with people that wouldn't honor their contracts to me, but I was obligated to fulfill my contract to you. I was both depressed and overwhelmed without any support, except from Belinda, but she was getting pretty tired of no money coming in for the work I was doing." Belinda interjected that that was the hardest time in their marriage. Potter said:

> There was a time when I was working from 6:00 AM to noon at your house, which I had exhausted all budgets, winging it as much as I could. Then I was working for Dave from noon to 6:00 or 7:00 at night and putting that money back into your house to get that house built. One day, I had gotten $40 in cash from Dave and I stopped someplace on the way home and lost the $40. I remember telling Belinda that I'd lost the $40, and we were devastated. That was all the money we had for the week.

Belinda's comment struck me: "I know it was hard, but I'd love to see you go back to something you love like that."

I know we were fortunate to have someone of Potter's integrity. When the roofer quit in a fit of pique, Carson Daley took over. "He wasn't a guy who got the architecture," said Potter, "but he was a guy who was willing to help me out for whatever I could afford to pay him." Here's the story: "Art came out when we were doing the shingles on the front of the house and stopped the job because the shingles were set very uniform, just straight across in rigid rows. Carson was mad—he said, 'You don't have the money to do that.' I said, 'I know I don't have the money to do that, but that's what I said I would do, so we have to do it.'" Potter understood the wave pattern Dyson intended and explained it, but Carson had lain the shingles in straight rows to save material and time. "We pulled off the section and put it back on per Dyson's drawing." By the time I got home from school, Carson was sitting out on the lawn in a chair, with the elevation of the front of the house spread across his knees, hands shielding his eyes from the light as he directed his nephews where to place the shingles—"up, up—now down—no, lower—now up." Potter explained it took three times the materials to create that layered look. Of course, the shingled front is a focal feature of the house.

Curving and overlapping as it does, the shingled front attracted bats (whom we appreciate for their mosquito-eating) and other creatures, great and small. We set Dani's crib in the upstairs loft room, which has a closet, but the closet was still empty. One day, I opened the closet door to find a fistful of animal bones on the carpet—I was mildly horrified until (and even after) I realized it had to be an owl roosting above the closet until we patched a gap between the attic and the closet and the house was owl-free.

Patience is a prerequisite for clients with creative projects. I have to point this out, even as I'm making the point that the time is worth it in the long run. We waited an entire summer for that front door (for a teacher, summers are the hardest time to wait because days are less structured). Potter built the masterpiece of a door by hand off-site in his brother's cabinet shop while working off-site to keep up with his contract. All in all, the 1800-square-foot house took 18 months to complete.

When the children grew up and we needed more space so brother and sister didn't have to share a bedroom, we talked about adding on. But I couldn't relinquish the original design. Years later, at dinner with the Dysons and Zimmermans, I was mystified by this conversation. I still can't picture how the design would work:

Art: Do you remember the addition we designed for this place?

Deb: We never...(shaking my head).

Art: But we designed one, maybe a couple of options.

Ann: Didn't it extend off the living room?

Art: We designed a second family room.

Ann: Extending out through a tube.

Deb: A tube? Like a Habitrail?

Ann: You could decorate it with tan shag carpet to resemble wood shavings!

Art: It shot out where that wall is (the woodstove wall) and it was the shape of the house in reverse; in other words, the form became the plan.

Deb: I don't remember seeing this—I remember asking if it was possible to add on…to create another child's bedroom.

Art: And it was all south glass; I don't know where the drawings are.

Deb: Were we so resistant to the idea that I don't remember it? How would the roof intersect with these angles?

Art: I think the roof went off at an angle toward the forest; it was elliptical, like a leaf. There was a glassed-in bridge area going across to it.

Ann: So the adults could be in this area, and the kids could go crazy in that area.

Art: Or the opposite.

Dyson's associate Rowan Hernandez later corroborated the story of the Habitrail addition. I suspect Dennis never shared this idea with me, having made up his mind to move to the Ranch House. He likely saw the design, thought "no way," and never let me see it, fearing I'd want to proceed. Hernandez described the other option as well—a bridge from the balcony upstairs to a master suite tree house in the forest canopy. The current master would have become a kid's bedroom. This story underscores the architect's point that you can only bring a client so far!

I agreed to leave the Dyson house the first time on the condition I could open out the interior walls of the Ranch House. In 1994, Boback Emad, following his apprenticeship with Dyson, was branching into design-build himself, so we all worked together, designing, building, and paying cash as we went. The plans the County approved were accurate, but simplified. We took the walls between the kitchen and dining room down to studs and made a round table out of cardboard to calculate the scale. We marked out the pool placement with a wobbly line of white flour.

It's to a client's benefit to have someone from the architect's circle on site, especially if the job is unique. Harvey Ferrero said most builders are reticent to attempt the unconventional. "And then a lot of builders don't like to work with architects, especially an architect like Art, because either an apprentice or someone who works for his office, or Art himself, will always be out on the job and make sure that contractor does what you want them to do." Ferrero said, "Most builders will take a look at the plan, and they'll roll the drawings up, and they'll put it in their back pocket and do pretty much whatever they want to do." He said most artist-architects will not do a job unless they can supervise so they do have control. Rowan Hernandez said owners who understand the architect's design can do deputy oversight. He said Dyson client Ken Woods kept plans handy. "When the shell was up, we'd go through, and he'd point out things that could be done better." On the RiverHouse, Mukai hired a worker to help with framing windows one day. I drove up just as the young guy was finishing the slot window by the front door— on a diagonal. I called Art, who confirmed it had to be horizontal and had to be re-framed. To Ferrero's point, Hernandez, who was a draftsman in Dyson's office, says, "He's very good at staying his ground. He's not offensive about it; he's very convincing because of his conviction, which a lot of people don't have. Hernandez commented how difficult some of the ideas were to execute. "[Dyson's] done a lot with 30/60-degree angles, but then he did some projects with curves [both my houses], and we had trouble getting computers to work with curves—he didn't draw a clean radius—there were sections of curves, like a leaf." And, of course, the truss company says it's more for every new curve.

Above: *Sid Mukai framing Lapp RiverHouse.*
Photo by Arthur Dyson.

Sid Mukai had worked on Dyson projects in the past, and he knows he'll "get bitten in the rear end if something's left unanswered on the plans." Permit granted in January, then it proceeded to rain for two months, during which time Mukai taught himself the CAD program Sketch-up. The longer it rained, the more detailed the drawing became, until we could see every angle, and Sid could use the computer model to explain to subs or the lumberyard exactly what it was he needed. Some of the decisions left to "figure out in the field" became clear as Sid entered them into the CAD program. "I'd thought some things were a little loose," Sid said, "but when I drew them up, I realized—he's a genius!"

Above: A soffit softens the angle in the Lapp RiverHouse bedroom.
Photo by David Swann.

Site visits from the architect can allow for tinkering with the design. As the walls were going up, I became agitated about the bedroom and its oppressive right angles. Your eye was drawn to one 90-degree corner, and your line of sight died there. Plus, our bed is low, and the ceiling was 18 feet up. How would reading lights work? I showed Dyson my idea of a soffit that would arc over the bed like a canopy, a convex circle. It articulated, I reasoned, with the convex half-circle of the terrace outside the mostly glass wall facing the river (that small terrace links to the larger terrace like a Venn diagram). The fan would be kind of squished in there, I admitted, but it could work. Art smiled and said simply, "Great, but make it concave." Dyson's inclination was so much better. The concave soffit looks like it was designed around the fan. Together with the convex half-circle visible through the glass wall, concave and convex arcs form a complete circle.

TOUR OF LAPP RIVERHOUSE

Once a year (when there's not a pandemic), we open the house to the public. I explain the history, the architect, and the planned elements of design, but I share all the building stories on this tour as well.

Still facing the front of the house, I point to the boulders that perch at the edge of the fountain and encourage people to notice that most of the decorations in the house and on the grounds originated on the property, emphasizing the connection to the natural elements that surround us.

For the mailbox post, Greg drilled center holes in river rocks the size of rugby balls and stacked them on a steel rod.

I point to the slot window in the aluminum pop-out. The pop-out has the effect of embracing the entry, just as the steel beams give it the impression of a low-ceiling entry. I show them also the swoosh etched into the front door frosted glass (I simply cut the design out of contact paper, backwards, applied it to the glass, and painted the stencil with the same acid the gangsters use to graffiti store windows).

I show them my wedding ring, which Greg and I designed to look like the river, and I tell them to look for the river swoosh motif elsewhere as we go inside.

The oversized door pivots. I close the door behind the last person to keep the bugs out and demonstrate how I lock it. Mukai was already puzzled with how to weatherstrip the edges when he suddenly stopped and said, "How are we going to lock it if it pulls closed with just a pole?" The ranchgirl in me answered immediately, "gate latch." And so it is.

As in the Zumwalt Residence, the low windows allow for cross-ventilation.

The heavy black parallel steel beams that run from outside in front to the pool on the back terrace serve not only to compress the 18-foot entry in a non-confining way, but also to connect the inside to the outside and balance the directional lines of the house. Without the north-south steel beams, east-west lines would dominate and make the design too static. The stunning east-west line begins with two massive glu-lam beams, which Mukai, after watching a documentary on the Hoover Dam, had placed with a crane in three segments: first east, then west, then center.

I tell them they're currently looking at three-quarters of the total house and remind them that the whole house is only 2,000 square feet.

In an *El Niño* year following some years of drought, a storm in late April offered us the opportunity to prove how nimble this house can be. The function was an 11:00 AM–3:00 PM barbecue / band / water activities / games sort of thing for about 200 people to benefit river programs and conservation. The heavens had dumped over three inches of glorious rain the night before and didn't stop until 10:30 AM that Saturday morning. Of course the band was worried about their equipment (their name was, ironically, Fire and Rain—of the two options, we Californians preferred rain). Tucked under the 15-foot overhang on the terrace, the musicians stayed dry, and the acoustics were better than ever. We moved

all the auction sheets and raffle prizes indoors, improvised seating, and set mats at every entrance. We covered the barbecue with tents like a bazaar and set the bar strategically near the auction tables. As the skies cleared, the games set up, and revelers played and listened to the band. People were in and out of the house all day, tracking soggy shoes of course, but the bamboo floors wiped right up and the house was back in order by dinnertime.

From the west wall behind the grand piano, I open one of the cupboards that together hold the 50 folding chairs. I explain that, with the furniture rearranged, it's easy to seat 50 people. The high counter above those cupboards, mostly bare, often holds stacks of music or chapters of works in progress.

From here, they are facing the window seat, reading nook, and library. Now they see how the slot window works at eye-height from a sitting position. In the earlier iteration of the RiverHouse design, the library was a separate room upstairs, but in the single-story version, the library is divided into three segments. Someone points out the river rock bookends. Someone else always asks, at this point, how we reach the beginning of the alphabet if Atwood, Borges, and Boyle are 16 feet up. The answer: telescoping ladder. I show my corner office, and open the drawer that has my laptop and pens.

Open and light-filled space for entertaining, a concert, or a yoga class.
Top photo by Ross Yukawa. Bottom photo by Greg Lapp.

I point out the terrace and the overhang stretching fifteen feet—more, if you measure the diagonal.

From this spot in the living room it's possible to see all five identical ceiling fans because above 8 feet, the walls are glass. This also allows for a continuous view of the glu-lams and ceiling that, without ducting for a dual-pack heater-air conditioner, curves smoothly in concert with the line of the roof.

In the kitchen, someone says they'd be glad to wash dishes here, and I have to admit the view does make all housework pleasant; I point out that it's an easy house to keep clean. There's a place for everything, so everything's in its place. One thing I've learned about open-format homes is the layout tends to sacrifice storage space, so in this house every wall and all the built-in furniture doubles as storage space or bookshelf, some of them 18 feet high.

I explain how, at the Creek House, which had an isthmus instead of an island, I could become trapped, my 6'4" husband blocking my escape. The circle of leatherized granite solves that, but it's too large to reach across. So Greg's father Leroy left the house one day with a trunkful of wood from an oak we had to fell and returned with the parquet lazy Susan for the center of the 8-foot island.

We didn't splurge on fancy appliances—nothing tricky—but we carefully planned the kitchen cabinets with Golden State Woodworking, down to the size of our biggest serving bowl and the height of the blender. So that a standard refrigerator could fit flush with the cabinets, we framed four feet of the wall deeper, intruding into the bedroom behind the bedroom door. This created a depression for a recessed bookshelf along the bedroom wall.

The wooden doors to the den, made by Greg and his father out of three woods, pull together the bamboo floor color (blonde), the piano and dining room table (cherry), and the front door and glu-lams (oak). They slide open and closed like a shoji screen. The edges are beveled, so they overlap for privacy as the room doubles as a guestroom. A framed rendering of the Creek House and a magazine ad for Kenwood stereos featuring the Creek House hang on the wall of the den, so I answer questions about that house.

In the den is the only window treatment in the house, blinds that close from the bottom up for privacy and to block the summer morning sun. Unless we have overnight guests, we leave them open the rest of the year. The TV is in this room, and the futon folds out. The whole house is wheelchair-accessible since Greg's brother uses a chair. The bathroom has accessible fixtures so Brian can stay here comfortably.

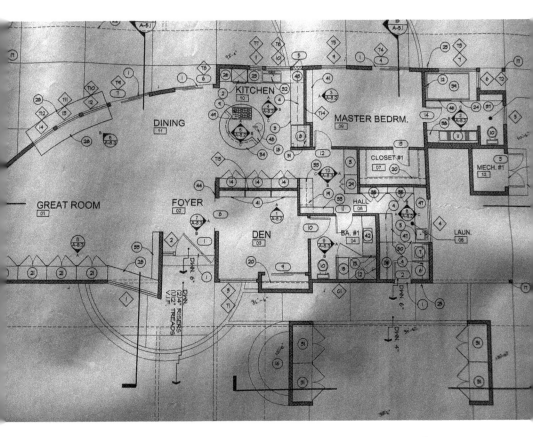

I send the group through the bathroom and the office/hallway and meet them in the bedroom. As they pass, I tell them to look at the poured concrete countertop inlaid with pebbles from the river. The bathrooms are all gray tile. It's nice that people think they are some special stone—they really *are* pretty—but they are ordinary tile, 16 x 16 on the floor and shower bench and walls, and 4 x 4 on the shower floor. The outside walls of the shower are glass, so the room looks bigger, and, like all the cabinet kicks in the house, there is an 8 x 8-inch clearance, so the cabinet looks like it's floating. The counter is deep, and the mirror meets flush with the concrete countertop, so the river rock design is doubled.

The office area is like a backstage view of our lives. There's the calendar, tickets and invitations, phone numbers and grocery lists, cookbooks, stationery, and a cleaning/linen closet.

Over the bed, feathers and dry flora compose a sort of dream catcher, found treasures from walks on the property.

Someone inevitably jokes about the glass shower walls, and I explain that the glare obscures the view, and from inside we see the river four times: the actual river through the east and north windows, the river reflected in the half-wall shower glass and then the glass door into the bathroom, and the 5 x 10-foot mirror behind the sink, which reflects all that glazing on the way back. To shower in the rain is to surround myself with falling water. In all weather, window glass, interior glass, and the ceiling-high counter mirror reflect the river in all directions. But on a May morning in a dry year, a welcome cool spell ushers in thunderstorms, and the cool shower outside coincides with a warm shower inside.

The poured concrete counter tops in the bathrooms began with hand-selected river pebbles glued in the swoosh motif of a streambed. We put down Styrofoam forms for the basins, Eddie Garcia poured the concrete and, once it cured, ground it smooth, but not too smooth where the rocks are because we wanted it to resemble a riverbed coursing across the counter.

Matt Taylor said something when he was touring the Lapp RiverHouse: the client continues the process, he said, of creating the built space by the choices he or she makes. He was referring at the time to a rock garden populated with round river boulders and outtakes from the glu-lam beams, which I set upright to look like river reeds and rushes flanking a steel heron I'd bought on impulse years ago. With the actual river beyond, it looks like he's just lifted his head from fishing. "The house may be finished," he said, "but you continue to create as you live in it."

I lead the tour back through the bedroom through the laundry room with a storage system that goes up to the ceiling, the printer and modem, sink, washer and dryer, outerwear closet, and a counter where Greg sets his school and music things. He also has a desk and piano keyboard in a studio upstairs in the barn (called the Tree House because its windows look out into the oak canopy). The Tree House also has a studio apartment with a small heat and AC wall unit for 110 degree days. Downstairs in the barn is Greg's shop and brewery.

Out in the carport, I explain that I didn't want a garage that would collect clutter. As in the house, the walls of the carport are deep storage cabinets, one side for sporting equipment and the guts of the fountain, the other for large-scale entertaining supplies.

Attached to the carport is an outdoor project room that also holds a freezer, the bicycles, and an exercise bike, all under cover.

Once Greg started making wine from his grapes, he needed a place to store it (my father had suggested as much when we were designing, but the budget didn't allow).

Ideally we would have dug into a hill. The highest hill area, though, faces the river, so it would be temptingly obvious to river floaters and park guests. The hill we chose on higher ground (good) is riddled with boulders (bad). This hamlet is called Piedra for a reason (*piedra* means stone in Spanish).

We rented an excavator, and Greg dug while I carted the dirt and rocks away with the tractor. When he ran into three boulders that wouldn't budge, he had to stop; we were just pleased that their crowns were relatively level, and we flattened out a level pad.

Greg found on Craigslist: 1) an airtight shipping container, and 2) a disassembled walk-in fruit refrigerator. We hired someone to deliver the container, who slipped it in on a dime. We encased the whole thing in fridge panels, saving the cleanest panels to make a solid floor. Greg pink-insulated the inside and covered it with Sheetrock to contain the cool. He built racks and shelves and left one 8 x 20-foot wall for me. Crowd-sourcing from my friends, some of whom are involved in the wine business or hospitality, I collected corks. Greg cut them in half with a band saw, and I glued them into a mural loosely based on sun, wind, and water. We don't actually hang out in there as there's not a lot of extra oxygen, but it's working well for wine storage, holding constant at 62 degrees.

At the end of the tour, someone usually asks what I would do differently—a good question. I remind them of the curved bank of windows in the living room and say that if the westernmost were partially openable, we'd have a better cross-draft. Someday, we'll split that window and the lower 24 inches will open with a screen for ventilation. The other problem we encounter is the sun, between 5:00 and 6:00 PM on summer evenings. We simply miscalculated, since the overhang deflects the sun for most of the day, and the sycamores pick up the slack in the evening, but there's an hour's gap. We toyed with some elaborate shade ideas, especially after visiting Zaha Hadid's Maxxi in Rome with its draping white shade cloth. But we realized that standard heavy-duty market umbrellas with the tilt feature could do the trick and move from place to place depending on the weather problem. We are powerless in the face of changing weather, so we're all going to have to adapt. ■

CHAPTER EIGHT:
SCULPTURE IN
THE FOREST

Above: The Lencioni Creek House with blooming wisteria.
Photo courtesy of the author.

"Animals arrived, liked the look of the place, took up their quarters, settled down, spread, and flourished. They didn't bother themselves about the past—they never do; they're too busy."

—Kenneth Grahame, *Wind in the Willows*

Until the children settled down, we had been renting the Creek House as a "Secluded Forest Retreat" on VRBO. I thought settling down might take awhile, since Nick is a Special Forces medic, a job that moves him all over the globe, and Dani and her husband are living a creative life in New York. They are now older than I was when we built the Creek House.

Guests who are artists articulate what they find beautiful about it, and most guests remark that the Creek House is "cool," both aesthetically and climatically. One artist-guest, a sculptor, quoted Ezra Pound: "I stood still and was a tree amid the wood and knew things unseen before," and he left a haiku in the guestbook:

Oak branch circles back

To leave a cursive message

Just after first light.

The angled windows spotlight wild bouquets and freestyle ikebana. The morning light, especially, dances across the floor and makes you glad you're up and alive.

From the rural road, North Rio Vista, our driveway, lined with figs and wild honeysuckle, winds into a clearing. The house—a sculpture, really—always surprises me, even after 30 years, and people often gasp the first time they come around the corner.

Art loves to tell the story of my son's kindergarten assignment to draw a house.

Above: One of Nico's house drawings (age four).
Photo courtesy of the author.

The way Art tells the story, Nico drew a building the shape of an eye with a circular door and a wild swoop projecting from the roof (similar to the even older drawing in the photo).

When the teacher called home concerned that he wasn't following directions, he says I invited her for coffee to see for herself the house that one friend calls "The Paisley" and my sister calls "The Eye." Our Egyptian exchange student said it was the Eye of Horace, a symbol of protection. A group of friends familiar with the house because we've met monthly since 1991, had seen it called "The Wave House" on HGTV's *Extreme Homes*. "Is it actually named the Wave House?" Susan asked, "I think it's more of a Mushroom." Linda calls it a Snail. In an interview, Effie Casey from Taliesin called it a Wooden Shell. Our prosaic names for our various spaces—Creek House, Ranch House, RiverHouse, Tree House—are really just for reference.

The November 25, 2012, episode of *Extreme Homes* featured a wide variety of buildings, as usual. The bumper music between the Italian makeover and the Lencioni Residence (Creek House) is a pounding boom-unh-

Above: Lencioni Creek House, from the south in winter
Photo courtesy of the author.

boom-boom, opening with blackberry bushes in the foreground and the house half-revealed behind. The enthusiastic voiceover announces: "Now, we're headed to a house, which, at first glance looks like Noah's Ark ran aground in Central California!" The camera follows the overlapping curves of the front shingles and rests on a section dappled by sunlight. He continues: "But the beautifully curved wood-shingled roof isn't just for looks. It's part of a design plan engineered to help this house stand up to a couple of the state's natural disasters—earthquakes and floods" (Boom-unh-boom-boom).

It's an incredible blue-sky day and the cottonwoods are in full shimmer. The announcer continues: "Dyson's clients wanted a home with high ceilings and big open spaces." Cut to the front of the house as the light shines on the lawn and forest. They interviewed Dyson on the site. "They actually had drawn a plan and had drawn an elevation," our architect begins. "They wanted a two-story," Art tells the camera, "and they came up with an A-frame." At this point a cool bubble lens swivels its view from the upstairs bedroom down to the great room below.

Above: *Lencioni Creek House "great" room.*
Photo by Scot Zimmerman.

Above: Lencioni Creek House from the east.
Photo by Scot Zimmerman.

The voice-over explains the flood plane regulations that require the house to be built up 3½ feet from grade. Art uses his hands to explain how he met the challenges of the site requirements. "We started tweaking things and pushing things out a bit—and then I learned that they liked curves."

The music changes to a bluegrass tune, and they capture some artistic shots of light and shadow, a view through the front door and the back windows to the forest.

"That's how the roof evolved from a big point that went up too high to this design terminating in an arch."

"The roof, made from red cedarwood shingle is composed of two huge interlocking curves. The upper curve allows for more interior space, while the inverted lower curve provides a visual counterpoint to the arching roof by swinging down to the flood-proof foundation. Plus, the shape of these locked curves is very stable, providing extra support against the shock of an earthquake." Here, they capture a wonderful evening shot

*Above: Lencioni Creek House back deck, raised for flood plane.
Photo by Scot Zimmerman.*

of the deck and the house lit up through the back windows. The lens must be a special wide-angle because, to me, it appears the photographer shoots from deep in the berry brambles. The figs and sycamore leaves frame the shot—similar to photo above.

The voice continues as the camera returns to the interior, showcasing the steel and wooden chevrons of the banister: "Inside, the home is not large, but, because the interior is almost entirely one room with a 21-foot-high ceiling, it feels like a much bigger space." Art explains, "It's a great room in the sense that it has the entry, the dining room, the kitchen, the living space all in one, but it's a very small great room." To illustrate, the camera travels from area to area showing the kitchen and breakfast bar, living room, looking over the sofa to the deck outside, dining room, also focusing on the view to the forest.

Above: Lencioni Creek House dining area.
Photo by Scot Zimmerman.

Above: Lencioni Creek House, view from the entry to the deck.
Photo by Scot Zimmerman.

Above: Parents' bedroom and balcony, Creek House.
Photo by Scot Zimmerman.

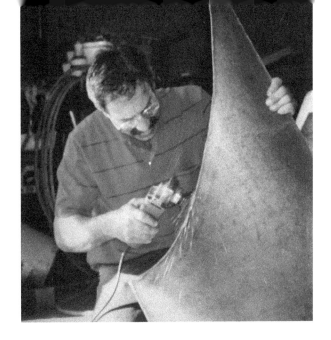

Above: Dennis Lencioni grinding a form for the fireproof shop.
Photo courtesy of the author.

The bluegrass music leads out to the deck, and they capture the details of the wood slats on the fascia reflected in the glass. "On the second floor is the study loft and a small den [office]," says the announcer as the camera pans around. This points out to me how flexible that loft space is, as it's been an art studio, nursery, library, playroom, teenage girl's bedroom, all with a view to the forest. "The two levels have very few internal walls separating them," he points out. The camera becomes mesmerized with the lighted etched glass under the stairs before describing the "eye-catching balustrade that would allow the homeowner, a blacksmith, to show off his skills."

Art tells the story. "We came up with a design, and I showed it to [Dennis]. He said, 'When I told you I knew how to weld, I meant I can attach two pieces of metal. I'm not a craftsman.' As you can see, he really rose to the occasion."

I'm still pondering the next statement: "The open plan, the high gallery, the curved beams give the building a feeling of a medieval hall..." (medieval hall?) "...but one well-suited for California's quake and flood country," and the last twang of the guitar resonates as a time-lapse photo of the sun sets in 80 brief frames. When the sun catches the sliver of a kitchen window and

Above: *View from the loft to the balustrade and forest beyond.*
Photo by David Swann.

creates a fireball, the photographer lets it over-expose and flood into oblivion, resolving impressively on the Cor-Ten rust wall of the next "extreme" home.

Steve Danforth, of the Wrightian Association, produced a video magazine called *Wrightian OA* (for Organic Architecture), funded by the Graham Foundation. The fifth of the series toured some of Arthur Dyson's works.

Above: *A fish-eye view of the "great" room.*
Photo by David Swann.

For the establishing shot, the camera pans the Fresno Art Museum exhibit of artifacts of Dyson designs such as cardboard models, a plant stand from the Manteca Church of Christ, a chandelier from the Baughman house, an extra balustrade segment Dennis had made for the exhibit. On the video, Dyson interprets several of the homes, and then the lens descends on the Lencioni Residence (Creek House). Dyson explains some of the cost-effective elements of the house. "Because it's a small space," he explains, "the walls are perforated and opened to expand the area." Dyson explains that the shingles on north and south were placed "in varying courses and widths to accentuate the sensuous lines of the house." And he explained how the builder (Greg Potter) chalked out the lines for the shinglers to follow.

Above: *Creek House kitchen.*
Photo by Scot Zimmerman

Art explains the "skyward-directed windows" of the fireproof shop, which Dennis had fabricated out of steel tubes welded together, and glazed with Lexan, which allowed some bending—"not all of them are flat planes," Art adds.

Then the camerman asks us about the design. "We were surprised and happy," says Dennis cautiously. "We pretty much trusted him with design. There were some complicated and trying times, but we thought the end product would be worth it." The interviewer caught us both in an unguarded response, and we answer almost in unison: "It isn't like you can go backwards after you see an Art Dyson design."

Above: Lexan skylights over fireproof shop.
Photo courtesy of the author.

The Creek House is like a wildlife blind. From the kitchen windows, I've watched herons gigging for frogs, a family of bobcats, quail bobbing up the drive. One time, when Dani was home from college, we were talking in the kitchen and a full-sized deer surprised herself as much as us by bounding from the thicket onto the lawn.

One challenge of the house, temporary resident Kristine Walter points out, was furnishing it: "It's not for someone who's rigid about having a sofa, two overstuffed chairs, and a coffee table. In this house, you need something that can move for the different purposes of the room." A stylish decorator, she has modular cubes in her current home, which she

Above: *Inside the one-cook kitchen.*
Photo by Scot Zimmerman.

says would have worked. She found the small cupboards in the kitchen frustrating: "I could never remember what I put in which little cubby." She said that, for a family, there's not much privacy, nor will it suit a person with lots of "stuff." She said it was a challenge to pare down to the essentials, but she said that editing process was healthy for her.

There were a few wonderful renters over 10 years. There was the violinist/ nurse with a newborn. Downstairs was nothing but a table, two kitchen chairs and a music stand, upstairs just a bed and a crib. A doctor in transition stayed there a year. Once, Dennis visited him in his office, and there was a photo of the Creek House on his wall.

Above: *The view from the forest.*
Photo by Scot Zimmerman.

Above: Photo by Scot Zimmerman.

Newly wed and newly hired to teach English at Reedley College, poet David Dominguez brought his new wife Alma to live in the Creek House for a year. Alma remarked that even though she was young, in her early twenties, when David went out of town once for a few days, she was never scared. She liked being surrounded by wildlife; she loved listening to the forest. One time she came to the door to say goodbye to David as he left for work, and right behind him on the other side of the fence was a bobcat. "One time, we were watching TV, and a fox walked right up the stairs and came up to the slider like it was no big deal. Elwood the cat was underneath the bench outside: the two just looked at each other, kind of nodded heads, 'How's it goin'? Nice night. Yeah—people are inside—humans.'" At their house in the suburbs, they have tried to recreate the forest by planting blackberries on two sides of the yard and fig trees.

It's no surprise that Dominguez wrote poems here for his new bride. Dennis and I had also been newlyweds in the house. We'd hang a mosquito net and sleep out on the balcony when the weather was balmy. David allowed me to reprint two poems that originally appeared in *Askew* literary journal, and his second poetry collection *The Ghost of Cesar Chavez* (C&R Press).

SONG FOR MY BELOVED

—The Song of Songs 4:1–2

The melting snow collects in the creek

surrounding the house my wife and I are leaving forever.

Cattails are singing, and the moon

slows its trip around the earth to listen.

I don't like being sentimental,

but tonight, I can't help it, so I tell her,

"Your hair is like a flock of goats."

My wife stretches her limbs on the blanket,

and I know she wants more.

Yerba mansa growing along the water's edge

blinds the willow looking for a place to root.

"I don't want to move," she says.

She asks impossible questions: "Will we be happy?"

I'm watching the current ripple over

pebbles lining the creek bed.

I wish the moon was a handful of bones

that the owl in the oak could read:

two hoots mean "no," and one hoot means "yes."

"Tell me about my mouth," she says, bending her wrist.

"Your teeth are like a flock of ewes."

I splash water onto her face and look downstream

where broken willow bounces along

the mud-caked bank.

David explained how hard it was to leave: "My 86-year-old aunt, when she goes into a room and begins to paint, she feels like somebody special is with her. She's talking about ghosts. She's talking about her mother. She's talking about her father. She's talking about the monks that she sees at night. She says they are with her. When she starts to paint, she feels as if she's in a secluded room where nothing can touch her. When she's done painting and she closes the door, she says every single time she feels she's lost a part of herself in the room. That's what it was like living here."

LEAVING SANGER

At night, my wife and I open the French doors,

slip into bed, and let the maple trees saturate the room.

Once, as the balcony filled with stars,

my beloved told me about her day:

how she saw a vixen and its kits reaching into a fig,

eat until plump, and skitter down a fence post,

and when the troop was safe,

the mother stared at my wife, its pupils warm in the light.

I can't say, "We won't miss it here,"

but the ranch will never be ours,

something my tenant heart forgets

when bullfrogs in the swamp begin croaking—

the rise and fall of a song soothing

as crickets grinding their legs under the leaves.

When Nico was 22 and going by "Nick," visiting the Creek House on leave from the Army, I asked him to draw a house to see what he'd come up with. He sketched the default peaked-roof, right-angled structure with symmetrical windows for eyes and the mouth a centered door. Yet, when we were talking about it, he paused, looked up at the curved ceiling and swooped his buff, tattooed arm over his head in an arc. "There was that day in kindergarten when Mrs. Varner asked us to draw a house, and I drew it like this." He repeated the curve over his head.

In the *Fresno Bee* recently, Donald Munro retold Dyson's story: "Lapp's son depicted a structure shaped like something you'd kick through a pair of goal posts. The teacher scolded him for fooling around." I received emails and comments from people co-opting this story as an example of how public education discourages creativity and encourages conformity. There might be something to that argument, but Nico was honestly never held back in his early grades at Centerville School. And, while the house is curved and pointed on both ends, I reject "Football House" as a nickname. It is an organic form, neither plastic nor pigskin.

Above: Of the front door, when we commented that it was reminiscent of a peace sign, Art shrugged and said he could design something more militaristic if we liked. Photo courtesy of the author.

Left: From the entry to the stairway. Photo by Scot Zimmerman.
Right: From the upstairs bedroom, looking out. Photo by Matt Taylor.

Actually, Harvey Ferrero told me a story similar to Art's about Goff's spiral-shaped Bavinger House: "It seems one of the Bavinger kids' teachers had him draw a house; when he drew a facsimile of the Goff design, the teacher's response was, 'That's not a house!'" Ferrero laughed and said that was clearly an opportunity for the teacher to come see where the child lived!

In this house, corners don't die into right angles; lines meander and curve and continue the whole length of the house, inside and outside; ideas and conversations are likewise unrestrained. When I spoke to her in 2011, Taliesin sculptor Heloise Christa praised Dyson for his "feeling for space," which she says is a rare gift, and she retold a story about him teaching his granddaughter Haley the concept of spatial relationships by arranging and rearranging chairs in a room. In fact, we designed and built chairs on wheels, so they could roll in the right direction for the moment.

Videos of architecture strive to show what can't be covered in a still photograph, the spatial kinetic sense of a place. The most serious problem with photography is that it's still, whereas experiencing architecture is kinetic. Even video mutes the sense of experience. As Matt Taylor wrote in an email discussion about this topic: "Architecture is not a visual art. It is a fact-based experiential art. The camera encourages designs that go for the money shot to the detriment of the whole."

As I stand here typing in the RiverHouse main room, light is pulsing its way over and through a cloud to the south, and radiating into the clear window above the frosted front door, causing the reflection of the water from the fountain to dance on the ceiling, and simultaneously dance on the glass between the kitchen and the bedroom. And, simultaneously, through the north-facing window, the wind is blowing the surface of the pool to the east (upriver) while the river itself flows west—you get my point. It's alive as no photograph can be.

Of course, the time would come when we would sell the Creek House. As hard as it was to let this piece of me go, we retired in 2020 and no longer wanted to be tied down to landlording. In the midst of the COVID-19 pandemic, we had no idea how the market would respond, and who would appreciate this sculpture in the forest. Fortunately, our realtor Nader Asemi did appreciate it, promoted it by video online, and encouraged me to hold out for a good price. It sold the first week for full price cash, no conditions. ■

CHAPTER NINE:
LOVE SONG TO
OUR RIVERHOUSE

Above: *Lapp RiverHouse, afternoon light on wildflowers.*
Photo courtesy of the author.

"Shadows in this house hang confidently like art. Where water dances on the ceiling, There is the music of light. Seven windows and one wall Reflect a vase of wildflowers."

A friend who's been to the RiverHouse frequently came for dinner last night. Both of our husbands were busy, and our schedules have been keeping us apart, so she drove her little SUV up the hill after her last class. Stepping through the doorway, she emitted an involuntary sigh.

That's what this house is like.

It was almost 6:00 PM, and the evening sun painted the hills. The arched expanse of windows creates a cinematic sense that this is the landscape of a story. Of course every landscape is the backdrop for someone's story, and this is ours.

Even when the river's low and the hills are dry, light slides with such drama that people stop and wait—the way people who live in the flight path of an airport wait for planes to pass overhead. Our wait is slower and more luxurious; if it happened more than twice a day it would be way too distracting.

We brought our glasses to the chairs by the window. The sun's strength was crossed by a chill wind up the river, so we sat safely inside. We talked of art and film and Shakespeare and the dramas in our lives. The sound of the fountain masked what evening traffic comes home with the commuters. Other than that, it was just our voices—words and laughter and exclamations like the wisps of clouds outside that were turning pink and gray and finally disappearing.

Greg arrived home as she was leaving. He reminded her that the futon folds out, the doors to the den slide shut—she could wake up to the sun

Top: Sunrise view from the RiverHouse.
Bottom: Evening view from inside out. Both photos courtesy of the author.

Above: *The windows reflect and duplicate the art.*
Photo courtesy of the author.

sliding down the foothills, but she had to get back to the city. We said goodbye to our friend, then settled in ourselves to discuss the day.

Sleepless at 3:00 AM, on a night when my brain won't rest, I slip out of bed to the window seat. The bamboo floors are tight and quiet and heat radiates through them, comfortable on bare feet. Lightning stripes the sky from behind the hills in pulsing waves—no wonder I'm restless, but how fortunate I am to witness this silent show. The sky calms, and I settle down. A photograph can show you the nook, but it can't capture the space. I nest in pillows on the bench. An overhead light illuminates my book, but, tucked behind the library wall to my right, it can't interrupt Greg's sleep. Specific to me, perhaps, is the comfort of a library, the endless possibilities of stories and ideas, many old friends and mentors,

Above: *Armchair view out the river-facing window.*
Photo courtesy of the author.

and some acquaintances I want to know better. At my eye level is the slot of a window—at night, from this angle, it is an obsidian detail, but in an hour, the hills will come slowly into focus.

The river windows across the room reflect me like a blurry negative, knees and shins, knees and shins, knees and shins, in triplicate. A confluence of angles and curves, this blending into that like a polyphonic motet, introduces endless possibilities of thought.

As the crickets' songs are replaced by those of morning birds, the day slowly breaks and pieces itself back together.

Above: A red-tailed hawk on a foggy winter day.
Photo courtesy of the author.

Whether Greg sleeps on, leaves for work, or joins me, I watch the world wake and corral the thoughts, resolutions, and images that come in the night, drinking milky coffee to hurry them onto a page. Thoughts slide across the arched ceiling and re-circle back down the other side. I lay scraps of paper in stacks along the high counter for chapters or paragraphs, and sort projects in a row of wicker boxes under the bookshelf. With a laptop, I can float from perch to perch around the wide room as my mood, inclination, or 60 year-old back determine. I try to channel patience, not from the busy finches, but from the red-tailed hawk, deep in concentration at the top of the sycamore.

Above: *The view from* shivasana.
Photo courtesy of the author.

There's a lull, and maybe an osprey flies past. Once I'm staring at raptors, not recording dreams and ideas, I stop to stretch my body with an online yogi. All the while, the sun reaches down the hill and into the water. The river surface skips upstream or down depending on the wind or lack of it. When the river is full and the current and wind are both strong, the river flows downstream (as it should) right to left, and the wind whips the pool water left to right. The illusion is a whirlpool. On a windy winter morning, the surface water flows upriver toward its source in Kings Canyon. "*Namaste,*" says the soothing voice.

Above: David Clemensen in concert.
Photo courtesy of the author.

On a June evening, birdsong comes from the piano. Thirty guests taste wine and cheese while our good friend David Clemensen plays songs, traditional and avant-garde, about birds: Daquin's "Le Coucou" (1735) and "Le Merle Noir" (1985) by Messiaen. We smile when a bird outside joins in. David plays river songs: Aaron Copland, Franz Schubert, Nico Muhly. He plays "Three Songs for the Kings River" by his friend Greg Lapp, a Frederic Chopin, John Cage, and Paul Simon's "Bridge over Troubled Water."

The acoustics of the curved ceiling create a surround-sound effect, blending the music as it originated in the composer's ear. One friend

for Deb and David. My two best friends.

Three Songs for the Kings

Text by Deborah L. Lapp
Music by Greg A. Lapp

says afterward, indicating the room, the view, the piano, "I feel like I've just fed my soul." Another says, "The peace is astounding." I ask which piece, assuming he meant *piece* of music, and he clarifies: "'that-passeth-understanding' peace." Above is the first page of the song we wrote; the rest is in the appendix.

Above: *After the storm.*
Photo courtesy of the author.

Greg and I built this house for the two of us, our friends and families, parties and concerts, retreats for the choral groups Greg conducts, but also as a venue for arts and environmental charity events. We are committed to sharing our space and benefiting our community. For these events, furniture moves aside, folding chairs are pressed into service, umbrellas go up, depending on the event.

Stormwatch is mesmerizing in any season. While the house is only 2,000 square feet, 48 feet of windows face the river, some of them 18 feet high.

After a drought, rain takes on mythical mother-goddess proportions. The wind shakes the trees, and they dance with latent animation. Unless it's very cold—and usually in California it's not—we like to open the glass. Windows are, after all, for letting in the wind. As it courses from the back of the house and out the front, the wind charges the house with its energy.

When my dream was near the moon,

The white folds of its gown

Filled with yellow light.

The soles of its feet

Grew red.

Its hair filled

With certain blue crystallizations

From stars,

Not far off.

—Wallace Stevens,
from "Six Significant Landscapes" (no. IV)

Above: *A full rainbow over the Kings River. Photo by Greg Lapp.*
Opposite: *The Moon in Blue. Photo courtesy of the author.*

On a January morning, the moon is still shining when the sun comes up. I know this because from bed I can see the moon in the mirror by the glass wall as the warm nimbus of sleep evaporates and stalls near the ceiling until dark returns. At the same time, through the wall of glass, I see the sun illuminate just the top of the green foothill across the river. As the sun rises over the Sierras behind us, the light will slide down the hill as the moon slowly dissolves.

Top/Bottom: Foothills view in fall.
Opposite: The RiverHouse echoes the foothills. All photos courtesy of the author.

Looking back at the house from the river with the mountain behind, the RiverHouse is just another foothill, slope-curve-slope. But it's the fancy foothill.

While the hills are green or gold or red, occasionally white, and the mountains a purple-blue, the house is silver-gray with a smooth arc of white roof.

The wall of glass, practically the entire north side, attempts camouflage as it reflects the colors of the hills and trees. It can't shake the shine. Summer mornings and evenings, afternoons in the spring and fall, we live outside, mostly on the terrace. A wide cement bench, flanked by garden boxes of kitchen spices, defines its edge. Greg's vines and the garden grow beyond. Greg mows the slope and the "apron," as we call the lawn. He carefully avoids any poppies or lupine that persist. While barefoot is a bad idea beyond because of goats' heads, snakes, fire ants (it's the country in California), the terrace is a barefoot space.

Cooking is pleasure for both of us: Greg is sous and science—he chops and makes complicated cheeses, fermented vegetables, even beer and wine—I am sauce, soup, and sauté. In summer, all cooking is on the barbecue. The farm-to-table food we make is a joyful gift to our guests and to each other. Greg might make sourdough pizza crust and mozzarella cheese. We gather tomatoes for sauce, and arugula, eggplant, garlic and zucchini.

Standing on the concrete bench that divides the orderly from the wild,

My back to the soft glow of kitchen light and reflection,

Lifting my face to the scattered stars,

I listen.

My lean cat comes in from the hunt like a suggestion.

The grapes and tarragon grow, even in the starlight

And gather the stars' crisp breath.

Without white noise, nights are quiet here. On dark, clear winter nights, Polaris guides me into my dreams. When the full moon eclipses the stars, I watch for a while as the shadows glint on the white sycamore limbs, and, as my limbs settle, sleep predictably settles in too. ■

Top: *Farm-to-table meal on the terrace.*

Middle: *A dramatic sunrise at the RiverHouse.*

Bottom: *My "lean cat" from the poem.*

All photos courtesy of the author.

APPENDIX

Above: View of RiverHouse from across the river.
Photo courtesy of the author.

for Deb and David. My two best friends

Three Songs for the Kings

Text by Deborah L. Lapp
Music by Greg A. Lapp

SIX SIGNIFICANT LANDSCAPES by Wallace Stevens, 1916

I

An old man sits

In the shadow of a pine tree

In China.

He sees larkspur,

Blue and white,

At the edge of the shadow,

Move in the wind.

His beard moves in the wind.

The pine tree moves in the wind.

Thus water flows

Over weeds.

II

The night is of the colour

Of a woman's arm:

Night, the female,

Obscure,

Fragrant and supple,

Conceals herself.

A pool shines,

Like a bracelet

Shaken in a dance.

III

I measure myself

Against a tall tree.

I find that I am much taller,

For I reach right up to the sun,

With my eye;

And I reach to the shore of the sea

With my ear.

Nevertheless, I dislike

The way ants crawl

In and out of my shadow.

IV

When my dream was near the moon,

The white folds of its gown

Filled with yellow light.

The soles of its feet

Grew red.

Its hair filled

With certain blue crystallizations

From stars,

Not far off.

V

Not all the knives of the lamp-posts,

Nor the chisels of the long streets,

Nor the mallets of the domes

And high towers,

Can carve

What one star can carve,

Shining through the grape-leaves.

VI

Rationalists, wearing square hats,

Think, in square rooms,

Looking at the floor,

Looking at the ceiling.

They confine themselves

To right-angled triangles.

If they tried rhomboids,

Cones, waving lines, ellipses—

As, for example, the ellipse of the half-moon—

Rationalists would wear sombreros.

Above Both: *Lapp RiverHouse front and back.*
Both photos by Scot Zimmerman.

WORKS CITED

Armstrong, John and Alain de Botton. *Art as Therapy.*

"Arthur Dyson." *Architizer.* https://architizer.com/firms/arthur-dyson-architect/

Bachelard, Gaston. *Poetics of Space.* New York: Penguin, 2014.

Baughman, Frank. Personal interview.

Bosch, Karen. Personal interview.

Briarly Cornelia. Telephone interview.

——. *Tales of Taliesin.*

Brink, Larry. Telephone interview.

Burke, Kevin. Text interview, personal interview.

Casey, Carl. Personal interview.

Casey, Effie. Telephone interview.

Chelazzi, Giuliano. *L'Archittetura Meditiva.*

——. Personal interview.

Chesley, Kate. "Re: Gratitude." Email to Arthur Dyson. March 6, 2013.

Christa, Heloise. Telephone interview.

Cohen, Bronwen."Space to Develop: How Architecture Can Play a Vital Role in Young Children's Lives." 2010.

Coronado, Elva. Personal interview.

Danforth, Steve. "Three Homes by Arthur Dyson." *Wrightian OA,* Graham Foundation.

De Botton, Alain. *The Architecture of Happiness.*

DeOrian, Sarah. Personal interview.

Dominguez, David. "Leaving Sanger." *The Ghost of Cesar Chavez* (C&R Press).

——. "Song for My Beloved." *The Ghost of Cesar Chavez* (C&R Press).

Dyson, Arthur. "A Search for the Soul of Architecture."

——. Personal interviews.

Dyson, Marc. Personal interview.

Early, Susan. Personal interview.

Emad, Boback. Personal interview.

Evans, Ron. Personal interview.

Ferrero, Harvey. Telephone interview.

Gage, Lee. Personal interview.

Gould, Stan. Personal interview.

Green, Will. Personal interview.

Guaglione, Roseanne. Personal interview.

Goff, Bruce. *Outside the Pale*. University of Arkansas Press.

Hammons, Mark. *The Architecture of Arthur Dyson*.
    ——. Personal interview.
    ——. "To Architecture." The Architecture of Arthur Dyson. 1994.

Harwood, Barbara. *The Healing House*.

Hernandez, Rowan. Personal interview.

Hess, Alan. *Hyperwest*.
    ——. Essay. Micky Muenig (monogram).

Hilton, Leila. Personal interview.

Ivy, Robert Adams Jr. introduction to *Outside the Pale*. Bruce Goff.
    University of Arkansas Press.

Jaksha, Tom and Sue. Personal interview.

Julavits, Heidi. *The Folded Clock*.

Joye, Yannick. "Architectural Lessons from Environmental Psychology:
    The Case of Biophilic Architecture." 2006.

Kelly, Bill. Personal interview.

Kisner, Jordan. "The Big Empty." *Thin Places*.

Landis, Paula. Email to Arthur Dyson. Re: The Cootie-Catcher House.

Lapp, Deborah. "Surrounded by Sculpture: The Joy and Value of Organic Architecture" *Journal of the Taliesin Fellows*, ed. Michael Hawker, Oct. 2011.

Lapp, Greg. "Three Songs for the Kings River."

Leverich, Diane and Veldon. Personal interview.

Lucchesi, Ron. Personal interview.

"Matt Taylor, inventor." *San Francisco Institute of Architecture*. https://www.sfia.net/people/faculty/matt-taylor-inventor/

Montooth, Minerva. Personal interview.

Moore, Linda McCullogh. "Men Who Make Houses." *Sun Magazine*.

Moreno, Shonquis. "This House Tells the Time with an Oculus." *Dwell*. 16 Jan 2009. https://www.dwell.com/article/this-house-tells-the-time-with-an-oculus-00cd45af

Muennig, Mickey. Personal interview.

Mukai, Sidney. Personal interview.

Munro, Donald. *Fresno Bee*.

Oschatz, Robert. Email interview.

Pearson, David. *In Search of Natural Architecture*.

——. *New Organic Architecture*.

——. *Organic Architecture: The Other Modernism*.

Peck, Susan. Personal interview.

Potter. Greg. Personal interview.

Rappaport, Howard. Email.

Shandilya, Umang. "Using Less, Living More, and Being Natural." *Slideshare.net*. Dec. 28, 2014.

Sigala, James. Letter to the Editor. *The Fresno Bee* Jan. 16, 2005.

Smith, Karl Ashley. *Haiku House*.

——. *Fine Homebuilding*. Jan. 1990.

———. *L'Architettura.*

———. Personal interview.

Stevens, Wallace. "Six Significant Landscapes." *The Collected Poems of Wallace Stevens.* Vintage Books. 1990.

Stitt, Fred. Personal interview.

Susanka, Sarah. *The Not So Big House.*

Swann, David. Email re: "Thinking about Your Book." June 12, 2014.

Taylor, Matt. *Post-Usonian Project.*

———. Personal interview.

@tcboyle, "Elfin Cottage." March 14, 2019.

Walter, Kristine. Personal interview.

Wasserman, Jim. *The Fresno Bee.* Oct. 1995.

"The Wave House" HGTV's *Extreme Homes.* Nov. 25, 2012.

Wheeler, Deborah. *Walton Sun.* July, 2001.

Whiting, Henry. *At Nature's Edge: Frank Lloyd Wright's Artist Studio.*

Woods, Ken and Carolyn. Personal interview.

Wright, Eric Lloyd. Personal interview.

Wright, Frank Lloyd "Idea and Essence." 1958.

Zimmerman, Ann. Personal interview.

Zimmerman, Scot. Personal interview.

Zumwalt, Kirk and Terri. Personal interview.

ACKNOWLEDGMENTS

Above: *Image of Scot Zimmerman, photographer.*
Photo courtesy of the author.

have had so much support and encouragement over the years as I've tried to find the direction and expression for what I have to say about my amazing architectural experiences while juggling family, work, and change that encompass a full life.

Greg Lapp encouraged me early: "I'd be impressed if you would do that." Nick Lencioni said, "It's like the two houses are bookends for your ideas." Dani Lencioni traveled to Italy with me, translated interviews in Italian, and transcribed so many others. She and Greg were two of my first readers.

Arthur Dyson, of course, and everyone in his firm past and present have given me not only designs for my homes, but kindness and an education in architecture and design. Clients of Dyson's, his colleagues from Taliesin, and fellow apprentices of his under Wright and Goff have been so generous in their stories, comments, and guidance. Matt Taylor and Gail Taylor infused this project with a new energy borne of their indefatigable enthusiasm and thoughtfulness about design and an organic life.

Ann and Scot Zimmerman have provided photographs and friendship and unfathomable support over decades and all the chapters of my life, and I appreciate feedback from someone in the know.

Colleagues David and Deb Borofka are both critical readers and critical support in the architecture of my life.

Thank you all.

Printed in the USA
CPSIA information can be obtained
at www.ICGtesting.com
LVHW071549050923
757292LV00010B/174